Demons Unleashed

True Tales of Terror Wrought by the Occult

John Harker

Shadow Hills Publishing

"Am I walking toward something I should be running
away from?"

– Shirley Jackson, *The Haunting of Hill House*

Author's Note

Most of the following accounts are drawn from the Christian tradition, particularly Catholicism. This is not to say there aren't stories of evil spirits, demonic possessions, exorcists, and exorcisms in other religions and belief systems. There are, of course.

However, the Catholic Church has such an extensive and documented history of dealing with supernatural phenomena that access to such stories is easier to obtain and learn from. This focus is not intended to push any one religion, but simply to show the effectiveness of one way of dealing with demons. There are undoubtedly other means to the same end.

Finally, while the essence of these stories remains intact, some names, locations, and similar identifying details have been changed to protect the privacy of certain individuals who either witnessed or experienced these events.

Contents

Introduction

The Demonic Reckoning

When my first book of a similar title, *Evil Unleashed: True Tales of Spells Gone to Hell and Other Occult Disasters*, was published in 2016, interest in the occult was at an all-time high, and there was little indication it would stagnate or regress any time soon. Move ahead a few years into the pandemic of 2020-2021—a time when people were locked down, stressed out, and giving up—and the numbers started rising rapidly again. Part of it was accounted for by people who lost their faith in God and turned elsewhere for answers in an increasingly insane, dark, and dire world. Others found aspects of the occult to be therapeutic, be it through divination, meditation, crystal gazing, or spell casting. Then there were simply the curious. Cooped up with not much more than a computer or smartphone for companionship and entertainment, a sizable contingent took advantage of the myriad of occult materials available online and decided, "Why not?"

The result has been an astonishing increase in occult activity across the globe, fueled in large part by social media. WitchTok, a subsection of the TikTok app, has amassed over 52 billion views of its video posts. Over 8 million posts on Instagram bear the hashtag #witchcraft. And tens of thousands of YouTube channels are dedicated to occult subject matter. This is not to mention the plethora of podcasts, websites, phone apps, and, of course, books that are available to the aspiring adept.

With numbers like these, it's not surprising that the occult has become big business. The "psychic services industry"—which includes mediumship, palmistry, tarot card reading, astrology, animal communication, and other practices—is valued at $2.3 billion as of 2023. According to the industry research company IBISWorld, both revenue and market share for these services are projected to increase over the next five years.

Spellcasting has its own profitable niche, as well, with shops on Etsy and TikTok and the like offering a wide assortment of love spells, revenge spells, good luck spells, weight loss spells—you name it, there's a spell for it. Need a more permanent solution? One shop, whose owner/operator unabashedly claims to make deals with demons "so all my spells come true," has been known to offer a limited-time, half-price deal on a "Powerful Death Spell." Make your problem go away for good for the bargain price of $271.04.

Internet storefronts and social media accounts run by solo entrepreneurs aren't the only avenues of occult commerce. Most of the large mainstream chain stores are in on the action too. Barnes & Noble now sells more than 29,000 products under the category "New Age & Alternative Beliefs," including two hundred unique decks of tarot cards. A search at Walmart.com for "witchcraft supplies" comes back with 1,000+ results, ranging from spell books to witch starter kits.

Sadly, many of these products are intentionally marketed to young people, with witchcraft now a popular subject of children's fiction. In October 2023, *The New York Times* featured a trio of reviews spotlighting middle-grade novels centered on witchcraft, alongside six reviews of "Terrific Witchy" novels targeting teen readers. Among these was a review of a book about a group of teenage girls who delve into "magic that feels hungrier and darker than what they'd previously dabbled in" as they attempt to bring their deceased friend back to life.

Some may wonder why these facts and figures are something to be alarmed or sad about. After all, trends happen, tastes change, thinking evolves. The University of Exeter thinks so highly of the occult's value to society that it is now offering a master's degree program in "magic and occult science." Distinguishing itself from a famous literary school of witchcraft and wizardry (lest its detractors think the students will be waving magic wands and flying around on broomsticks), the university stresses that at the "core" of the coursework are the themes of "decolonization, the exploration of alternative epistemologies, feminism, and anti-racism."

With such lofty ideals as these, why should we be concerned? Aside from the casting of death spells, most occult practices seem pretty harmless. And for most people who dabble from time to time with things like Ouija boards or fortune telling, nothing much happens to them, at least as far as what's visible to the eye.

But that's the problem. It's not the visible but the invisible that we have to worry about. As the chief exorcist of the Diocese of Indianapolis, Father Vincent Lampert, explains:

"We must realize that a non-material world does exist with nonmaterial beings, namely, demons. These entities are the source of the power and knowledge displayed through the use of astrology, palm readings, tea leaf reading, tarot cards, spiritism (séances and automatic writing), pendulums, Santeria, Voodoo, potions, herbs, amulets, and crystals."

Just as the occult is all about hidden knowledge, the forces that supply its power prefer to remain hidden as well. After all, if every time a pack of tarot cards was opened, a demon popped up like the Genie in Aladdin, people would run away screaming. Or if a teen witch wannabe could see the actual netherworld entity delivering that love spell, she would maybe reconsider the TikTok channels she watches.

Instead, though, most occult activity is carried out without any concern of repercussions. For many, such activities are merely entertainment. In fact, many so-called occultists don't even believe in demons, angels, the devil, or God. They use the vague terms "Spirit" or "The Universe" to describe the "energy" source of their endeavors, and they obliviously stumble and bumble along, believing they are harnessing the secrets of the natural world.

Then, of course, there are the serious practitioners, the ones who know exactly who or what they're invoking when they cast their villainous spells and carry out their vile rituals. For reasons that are unfathomable, they freely choose to side with evil and accept its empty promises. Superficial rewards and transitory pleasure are enough to entrap some. Others have been ensnared for so long, that they fear trying to leave, as their debt is too high and the expected payback too horrifying.

Whether dabblers or devotees, practitioners of the occult eventually come to realize that actions have consequences. And in the case of our current societal state, the increased occult action, as evidenced by the statistics discussed earlier, has had as its consequence a staggering increase in the number of calls to exorcists. People from all over are reporting instances of demonic harassment, vexation, infestation, and even possession. Father Lampert, to cite just one example, received prior to the pandemic approximately 2,000 inquiries each year from people concerned about demonic troubles. Since 2020, he has received approximately 3,500 such inquiries per year.

Dr. Richard Gallagher, a board-certified psychiatrist and professor at New York Medical College and Columbia University who works with the Catholic Church in distinguishing genuine demonic possession from medical and psychological disorders, attributes the rising demand for exorcisms to two main factors: The first is an unprecedented preoccupation with the paranormal, driven by the constant offerings from television, movies, books, and the internet, which makes people think they need an exorcism when they don't. The other is the decline of traditional religious institutions and beliefs. As he states, "When people give up a mainstream or more orthodox type of religion, they generally develop some kind of substitute belief system. That often involves ideas about energy forces, occult themes, and visitation by spirits." Dr. Gallagher, who has seen his share of actual demonic possessions, further explains how many exorcists believe that "through alternate spiritualities, these people have opened themselves up to evil forces and evil spirits, in ways that more mainstream religious people are protected from."

Dr. Gallagher's views might draw negative reactions from the non-religious. There are undoubtedly instances of people who have immersed themselves in every type of New Age, occult, or pagan practice with little or no turmoil to their lives. They may appear, in fact, to be happier and healthier than many churchgoers. And they may be. Going to church won't in and of itself protect you from the demonic. But case after case shows that the occult offers no protection at all, and, more often than not, summons these terrible entities right to your door.

The cases in this book exemplify that reality. They also illustrate the difficult and sometimes treacherous steps people go through to rid themselves of their demonic foes once the battle has begun. If they can rid them at all.

I hope you will find these stories interesting and informative. I hope they impress upon you the evil and destructive natures of these spiritual creatures–these demons–that the dark arts unleash. But most importantly, I hope they will help banish any curiosity or inclination toward the occult, in any of its overt or disguised forms. I would prefer that my readers, their families, and friends, remain safe and healthy, in body, mind, and soul.

"There is pure evil that lurks in the universe just waiting for an invitation or opportunity to strike."

– Debi Chestnut, paranormal investigator and author

CHAPTER 1

Ouija Board Phantoms

There is one occult divination device that has caused more harm than perhaps any other: the Ouija board. Some statistics from paranormal investigators and exorcists report that over 80 percent of demonic possessions happen as a result of Ouija board interactions. Its power comes from presenting itself as a game, when in fact it is a gateway to a dark dimension that invites any and all denizens to cross over into our world. It may take days, weeks, or even years before an entity manifests after that door has been opened. But by then, the victim has let their guard down and becomes the very thing they considered the board: a plaything, but for a cruel and evil game master.

* * *

After a demanding work week, Amanda was more than ready to spend Friday night relaxing in front of the television. A dental hygienist by trade, she had had enough of looking into other people's mouths, and tonight she was only interested in pouring a glass of wine into her own. Her solitary plans were interrupted, however, when her roommate, Carly, came home early from her date. Carly's boyfriend, Rob, wasn't feeling well and sent her home in case he was contagious. "We were going to play around with this," she told Amanda, pulling from her bag what looked like a board game. "How about you

15

and I try it out?" Amanda could now see that the "game" was actually a Ouija board. She had heard about the Ouija from movies and social media but had never actually used one. Her curiosity was piqued. "Why not? I'll pour another glass of wine."

While nothing "supernatural" happened during their gameplay that night—much to their disappointment—strange occurrences did begin to bedevil the roommates afterward. For starters, their normally quiet abode was beset with loud footsteps in the hall and, remarkably, on the ceiling. It was almost as if someone was marching around in heavy work boots—except no one was ever visibly present. The girls would also hear the sound of wind chimes inside the house, which in itself wouldn't be too upsetting if there were wind chimes anywhere on the property, which there weren't.

Then one night things took a more frightening turn. Amanda was in bed reading by the dim light of a small lamp next to her bed. She felt herself getting tired, put the book aside, and stared off into space while waiting for sleep to overtake her. Just as she was about to close her eyes, she noticed a shadow in the corner of her room start to get darker and darker. The shadow grew larger and shifted in shape until it formed the silhouette of a person. Amanda felt her heart leap in her chest and, fully awake now, watched in terror as the shadow man slowly walked toward her. As he came closer to the light, she could tell he was wearing clothes from an older time period, although nothing on the figure was truly distinct, including his face, which remained featureless behind a vacillating black mass. Amanda tried to scream but her voice was paralyzed. Then, to her amazement and relief, the shadow figure passed by her bed and walked directly through her bedroom door out into the hallway. For several long minutes, Amanda lay still, fearful that the "thing" would reappear at any moment. Thankfully, it didn't, and eventually sleep overtook her.

But the shadow man was not gone for good. In the weeks that followed, both Amanda and Carly saw the black figure frequently, in the daytime as well as at night, silently slinking throughout all the rooms of the house. Sometimes it would stop and stare at the girls, sending chills down their spines, before it would inexplicably vanish into a wall or door. As the weeks turned into months, and without the financial resources to move, Amanda and Carly had no choice but to accept their spectral roommate as an unsettling but otherwise harmless presence.

For most people, living with one phantom would be quite enough. But soon a ghostly woman in a white gown began appearing occasionally, along with more regular visits from two young children, a boy and a girl. These phantom children weren't only visible to Amanda and Carly, but to guests as well. Amanda recalled one time overhearing her niece, who was staying the night, talking to someone in her bedroom. When she opened the door, she saw her niece on the floor by her dollhouse. The girl looked up at Amanda and said, "Where did he go?" When Amanda asked the girl who she was talking about, her niece answered, "The boy who was playing with me."

Carly saw the boy once standing next to Rob's car, almost as if he wanted a ride. And Rob heard the children giggling once while he was in the bathroom, making him uncomfortable about coming over to the house quite as much. Bathroom pranks seemed to be a favorite, as Amanda recalled one time having her hair lifted up while she was in the shower. Despite these strange occurrences, Amanda and Carly were still willing to co-exist with these additional spirit presences.

Until things took a darker turn.

After about a year of living in relative peace with the phantom figures, Amanda began having terrifying nightmares about shadow creatures chasing her through a desert. The dreams were so vivid that she could actually feel sand on her face when she woke up. The nightmares continued for six straight nights, but the real horror came afterward when she began seeing the shadows from her dreams following her around the house. There was no respite out in public, either, as she would see people around her with no whites in their eyes.

Amanda tried to convince herself that it was only her imagination getting the better of her, but one night in the shower, she broke down sobbing, overwhelmed by fear and anxiety. More and more, she had been thinking it wasn't just ghosts hanging around, but rather something more sinister. As water from the shower rained down on her, she screamed out loud, "Demons aren't real! Demons aren't real!" Suddenly, she began choking as if something was tightening itself around her throat from the inside. Though terrified, she sensed clearly that she needed to acknowledge that "demons *are* real" to make the attack stop. She sputtered the assertion and the choking ceased.

For several days after conceding the existence of the dark entities, Amanda experienced no further disturbances. She dared to hope that, as before, a peaceful co-existence was possible. It soon became apparent, however, that the other party was not going to play the same game. While alone one night, sitting on the couch, Amanda suddenly felt like something reached into her chest and grabbed her heart. The pain was immense, and for a moment she thought she was having a heart attack. But along with the very real pain, there was a palpable sense of evil all around her. A sense that someone, or something, was deliberately doing her harm. As the violence against her continued (she stated later that it was as if something was trying to pull her heart out of her chest), her Lakota upbringing revealed itself with a thunderous plea to the Great Spirit to spare her. At once, the pain began to subside.

In the days that followed, as much as Amanda wished that the spiritual help she invoked would last, more frightening incidents continued to happen to both her and Carly. Often they would hear scratching in the walls beside their beds and were frequently awakened by loud, hissing growls in their rooms. One night, just as she was about to fall asleep, Amanda heard people screaming and arguing in the hall. And Carly nearly broke her ankle jumping out of bed one night when her blankets were suddenly yanked off her by some unseen force.

By now, understandably, the women were at their wits' end and ready to enlist outside help. Carly had been taking night classes at the local community college and remembered seeing a flier for a guest lecture by a self-described paranormal investigator and demonologist. The girls immediately made plans to attend.

On the night of the lecture, Carly and Amanda sat enthralled as the speaker, Martin, described the various cases he had worked on over the years. Much of what he spoke about was eerily similar to what they had experienced, and after hearing about his incredible supernatural encounters, they no longer worried about appearing crazy themselves. They approached Martin after the talk and told him their story.

Sympathetic but forthright, Martin advised them that it was most likely their Ouija board session from over a year ago that inadvertently allowed these beings to enter this dimension and raise havoc. The first thing they had to do, he said, was get rid of the board, even if they hadn't used it since that first time. Now that it had been "activated," the board was not only a source of demonic attachment but also an open portal to the spirit world. Next, they needed to arrange for a spiritual "house cleaning," which the girls asked if he would do for them. He agreed and a date was set.

When Martin arrived later in the week, along with a woman named Ann who was a psychic sensitive, the first thing he made clear was that the girls needed to foster and continue a relationship with God, or the Great Spirit, as Amanda called Him. This will always break the bond that otherworldly Evil has made with a human, he explained. God is the Light, and just as we turn on a light to banish the dark from a room, so should we call on the Divine Light to banish darkness from our lives and our souls.

Then he and Ann went room to room, burning white sage, sprinkling blessed salt and holy water in every corner and at each doorway, and reciting prayers that commanded any and all evil entities to leave in the name of God. When they were done, Ann said that she could no longer feel the presence of any spirits. Amanda and Carly breathed a sigh of relief. Could it be possible that they were finally free after all this time?

In the days that followed, the girls noticed a significant change in the atmosphere of their home. The once heavy and oppressive feeling was gone, replaced with a palpable sense of peace and security. They no longer heard terrifying noises, saw mysterious phantom figures, or suffered attacks from invisible assailants. The darkness that the Ouija board had ushered in was truly gone, and the roommates were determined to keep it that way through living in faith and abiding in the Light.

"I like to compare people using an Ouija board to being a telemarketer—you're calling all these phone numbers and you have no idea what type of person is going to answer the phone. It is a very dangerous situation to be in."

– Samantha E. Harris, paranormal investigator and author

CHAPTER 2

An Exorcism in Africa

Troublesome and deceptive spirits have plagued humankind since the dawn of time. In Christianity, they are known as fallen angels or demons; in Judaism, they are identified as dybbuk; in Islam, they are referred to as djinn or shaitan; in certain branches of Buddhism, they are called animal spirits; and in Native American religions, their names vary by tribe. There also exists in each of these traditions some form of an exorcist—an individual who possesses the knowledge and authority to expel these spirits from those they afflict. Thankfully, such cases are typically rare, but when they do occur, they present a challenging and somewhat perilous endeavor for all involved. A successful deliverance makes it all worthwhile, of course, but success is not always guaranteed.

* * *

1910 in the Belgian Congo

In the dimly lit confessional, the young girl trembled with fear and shame. As she waited to hear the familiar sound of the wooden window sliding open, she wondered what Father Henri would think of her. Would he even grant her absolution, given the terrible thing she did? She closed her eyes tightly and clutched her rosary. The window slid open. Anna steadied herself and began the age-old penitential rite.

"Forgive me, Father, for I have sinned," she whispered, her voice barely audible in the heavily muffled compartment. "I have made a pact with the devil."

Father Henri, an older man with a gentle demeanor, remained silent for several moments, collecting his thoughts. He was familiar with the girl's tragic past: orphaned as a baby and taken in by the Divine Word mission school at the tender age of four. Despite her hardships, Anna had been a diligent student and devout Christian, leaving him to wonder what could have possibly driven her to such a dark confession. At last, he spoke.

"Child, you must understand that such claims are not to be taken lightly. Are you certain this is the truth?"

Anna nodded fervently, tears streaming down her cheeks. "Yes, Father. I did it. But now I can feel him inside me, controlling me, changing me."

"I see," the priest said. Thinking that the girl's confession was either a flight of fancy or perhaps even a cry for attention, he gave her the best pastoral advice he could. "Anna, the devil tries to tempt and trick all of us. Whatever you think you have done, you're rejecting his ploys now with your confession. Rest assured that with the Lord's forgiveness that I'll give you here in a moment, you will no longer be under his control. All right?"

Anna agreed and tried to take comfort in Father Henri's words of absolution, but as she left the confessional, she still felt weighed down by the secret act she had performed months earlier when she had been overwhelmed with feelings of anger over her past and anxiety over her future.

Nonetheless, she told herself she would try her best to shake off all thoughts of devilish dealings and resume her normal life activities. With a bit of a lighter step, she skipped down the path to the kitchen to help the nuns prepare for supper.

In the days that followed, however, life within the walls of the mission was anything but normal. Whispers spread among the nuns and the students as they observed a drastic shift in Anna's behavior. Once a model student, she now seemed consumed by an unseen force, physically struggling with herself in bizarre, even violent ways. She ripped at her clothes and screamed vulgarities. She contorted her body into unnatural poses and spoke in tongues that no one could understand. Most disturbingly, she would erupt in mocking, derisive laughter whenever the nuns prayed or sang hymns, showing no trace of her former reverence.

One day, several of the nuns found the girl huddled in a corner, engaged in a fervent conversation with the empty air. "Anna, what has come over you?" asked Sister Celine. "You must tell us what is happening."

"Can't you see them?" Anna cried out, her eyes wide with terror. "They're here, all around me! I can't escape them!"

The concerned nuns tried desperately to control Anna's shocking outbursts, but she only grew more erratic by the day. In addition to seeing demons, she also claimed that Satan spoke to her. On one occasion, while in a particularly distressed state, she answered back, "You have betrayed me! You promised me days of glory, but now you treat me cruelly."

One night, the nuns were jolted awake by the ghastly sounds of Anna barking and snarling on all fours like a rabid dog. Armed with rosaries and holy water, they circled around her, praying for her deliverance from whatever nefarious force they were now convinced held her in its control. After several heart-pounding minutes, Anna let out a plaintive moan and fell flat to the ground.

"Please," she gasped in a hoarse voice as she clutched at Sister Celine's sleeve. "You must get the priest or I shall not survive the night."

The nuns had seen enough to not doubt Anna's words. One of them ran off to fetch Father Henri while the others helped Anna to a chair. The young girl's eyes darted frantically about the room as if seeing danger in every corner. "He has me in his power!" she wailed. "I have no protection; I have thrown away all the blessed medals you gave me. Quick! Quick! Get the priest!"

The flickering candlelight cast eerie shadows across the walls of the otherwise dimly lit room as Anna sat huddled on a wooden chair, trembling uncontrollably. The sound of her ragged breathing echoed in the oppressive silence, punctuated only by the soft murmurs of prayer from the nuns who stood vigil around her. Finally, a new sound, that of hurrying footsteps, carried into the room. Father Henri rushed through the door and stopped short when he saw Anna in her disheveled state. She raised her head and stared back at him, her eyes burning with an unsettling intensity.

Father Henri had seen those eyes once before, years ago in another part of Africa. They had belonged to a possessed witch doctor who had openly and willingly invited demonic forces to enter and empower him. The same ancient evil was now present in Anna, of this the priest was certain. He stepped forward, made the sign of the cross over the girl, and began praying.

"Curse you!" she spat, her voice a guttural snarl. "You have no power over us."

As one of the nuns reached for a vial of holy water, Anna's gaze followed her hand with unnatural precision. A malevolent grin twisted her lips as she let out a scornful laugh that echoed through the halls.

"Go ahead," she hissed. "It will do nothing."

The nun hesitated for a moment, a flicker of doubt crossing her features before she steeled herself and sprinkled the water onto Anna's trembling form. The girl's scream was one of pure agony, her body arching up from the chair as though touched by searing flames.

"Begone, evil spirits, and leave this girl alone!" Father Henri boomed authoritatively.

Anna's screams of agony instantly turned into shrieks of laughter. Then she spoke unknown words in rapid succession, her tongue effortlessly weaving between languages that no sixteen-year-old should have been able to comprehend.

"Please, Lord, give us the strength to help this child," Father Henri prayed, his voice barely audible above the howling wind that seemed to have picked up outside the chapel's heavy doors.

"You will never have enough strength," Anna said in a deep, unearthly voice. "She is ours. She gave herself to us and we are never letting go."

And then, as if a switch had been triggered, Anna slumped in the chair, her chin resting on her chest, and all was quiet. After a minute, she looked up with eyes that were clear and innocent. "Where am I?" she asked bewilderedly. "What happened?"

The priest and nuns looked at each other, knowing that a bigger battle was indeed yet to be waged. Father Henri made haste to his office. He needed to write to the bishop immediately and get permission to do a formal exorcism. And he needed help as well. When the time came, it would be ugly and treacherous. He did not want to endanger the sisters, many of whom were elderly with weak hearts.

As the days turned into weeks, the once-serene mission was haunted by an ever-present sense of dread. The nuns found themselves plagued by nightmares and inexplicable fears, while Anna continued to exhibit increasingly alarming behaviors. And though they prayed fervently for her deliverance, it seemed as though their efforts were in vain.

Finally, on September 29th, the feast day of St. Michael the Archangel, having received permission from his bishop to perform an exorcism, Father Henri and a young visiting priest, Father Simon, prepared for the sacred rite in the mission chapel. Anna seemed in control of herself during the preparations, and she agreed to be tied to a chair to ensure the safety of all involved. A few of the younger, sturdier nuns stood by, ready to assist.

Reading from his ritual book, Father Henri began the exorcism. As the sing-song cadence of the Latin prayers echoed off the chapel walls, Anna's demeanor slowly began to change. She started to writhe under the restraint of the ropes, and girlish giggles bubbled from her mouth. Abruptly, she turned her head and locked eyes with the visibly nervous new priest, who clutched a Bible to his chest as he tried not to tremble.

Father Henri stepped closer and held up a crucifix six inches from Anna's face. In an authoritative voice, he ordered, "Ecce crucem Domino: fugite partes adversae!" (*Behold the Cross of the Lord: take flight, you hostile powers.*)

"Never!" came a gravelly response from Anna's lips. Her body convulsed violently, causing the wooden chair in which she was restrained to skitter across the floor.

"Father Henri, be careful," Father Simon warned.

"Silence, weakling!" the voice from Anna commanded. Then, in one swift movement, she broke her arms free from the ropes like they were mere threads and lunged for the young priest, knocking the Bible from his hands. She grabbed his stole and was attempting to strangle him with it when the nuns grabbed her and wrestled her to the floor.

"Your pathetic rituals cannot defeat me!" boasted the demon as it bucked wildly against the nuns' hold. "I will make this child my vile plaything for eternity!"

With renewed vigor, Father Henri resumed the ritual prayers, interspersing his recitation with douses of holy water upon the struggling, screeching girl. The air grew thick with the smell of sulfur as both priests now joined their voices together to drown out the demon's taunts.

"Your efforts are futile," Anna hissed, glaring at the two priests with the slit eyes of a snake. "You cannot save this wretched soul."

Then Anna's body went limp, her eyes returned to normal, and she looked around in confusion. "How did I get on the floor?"

Father Henri offered a reassuring nod to all present. "Some are gone, but the commanding demon is only dormant. Tomorrow, we shall try again."

As the first light of dawn filtered through the stained glass windows, casting kaleidoscopic patterns upon the chapel floor, Father Henri and Father Simon prepared for what they hoped to be the final confrontation with the evil residing in Anna. Knowing that ropes wouldn't hold her when the demon manifested, the priests this time marshaled the assistance of four burly men from the village to restrain Anna should it become necessary.

Which it did within a very short time. As the priests began the Litany of the Saints, Anna became a wild animal, thrashing about, shrieking and snarling. The village men struggled to restrain her, amazed at the strength of the frail-looking teenager in their grasp. For hours the battle raged on. Anna fought with preternatural fury against the words and actions of the priests. Crucifixes held before her face elicited screams of rage. Holy water brought forth shrieks of agony. At one point, she appeared to be choking on something, only to vomit up what looked to be the nails of a jungle cat.

After an eternity of bluster and chaos, Anna suddenly became quiet and still. Eager for a break, the exhausted men at her side made the mistake of relaxing their grips. With alarming alacrity, Anna slipped from their grasp and slithered down to the floor like a snake. Her eyes became slitted and her tongue, stretched to an impossible length, flickered in and out of her mouth in obscene gesticulations.

Undeterred and stone-faced, the priests continued the ritual. Though physically and emotionally drained, they knew they were close to driving out the fiend and would not stop now for anything.

"Reveal your true self, demon!" Father Henri demanded. "Provide a sign before you are cast out!"

"Very well, you hairless ape," a raspy voice replied, smirking through Anna's lips. "I will levitate this worthless body as my final show."

The men began to haul Anna back up to her chair, but Father Henri waved them back. A hush fell over the chapel as those who were gathered—priests, nuns, villagers—held their breath and fixed their eyes on the undulating girl. Suddenly, her body went rigid, extending itself like a wooden plank. Then, slowly, like a marionette controlled by an unseen puppeteer, her stiffened corpus began to rise from the floor.

"Lord, have mercy," Father Simon whispered.

Anna continued to rise three feet in the air before her body suddenly lost its rigidity and came crashing down to the ground. Sister Celine rushed over to Anna's crumpled, still body and cradled the girl's head in her lap. After several tense moments, Anna opened her eyes and began weeping tears of joy.

"Is she... free?" Father Simon asked hesitantly.

"Yes. It is over," Father Henri replied. "Praise be to God. But we must remain vigilant."

Father Henri's warning proved necessary. Less than a year later, Anna allegedly made another pact with the devil and another two-day exorcism followed. Historical records indicated that the exorcism was "successful," but no other information about Anna was ever documented. Her final fate remained as enigmatic as the entity that had once claimed dominion over her.

> *"Evil is Someone, Someone who is multiple and whose name is legion… It is one thing to be in the realm of the demons, as we all are when we have lost the state of grace, and quite another to be held and surrounded, literally possessed by him."*
>
> **– François Mauriac, Nobel Prize winner of Literature**

CHAPTER 3

A Cursed Vengeance

Witchcraft and sorcery have been present in the Philippines since long before the Spanish colonization. Mixed with the rich and varying traditions of indigenous folk religions, the practice of black magic is not only deeply embedded in the historical lore of the islands, but continues to be a flourishing business to this day, with some spells and curses going for upwards of $700. A steep price, indeed, and often paid for in more ways than one.

*　*　*

It was a beautiful, sun-drenched day in the Western Visayas region of the Philippines, and Reyna Santos's luxurious estate, right outside Iloilo City, was abuzz with activity. Loy, the gardener, was masterfully trimming bougainvillea and orchids into tidy spirals. Lita, the cook, was busy gathering handfuls of mint and basil for the widow's lunch. And Aurora, the maid, was just finishing tidying up the master suite.

In contrast to the opulence that surrounded her, Reyna Santos was shackled by frail health. A year after her husband's death, she was diagnosed with multiple sclerosis, confining her to limited activity, long periods of rest, and increased dependence on her staff. Her physical frailty, however, didn't hinder her sharp business sense, and she spent every morning going meticulously over the books of the sugarcane business her husband had worked so hard over the years to build.

A week prior, Reyna had discovered a discrepancy in the billings, and then another, and then another. All could be traced, unfortunately, to a plant foreman who just happened to be Aurora's nephew. As Reyna sat in her favorite chair in the solarium, soaking up the sun's energizing warmth, she worried how Aurora would take the news that Reyna had alerted the police to her relative's activities. She would soon find out, as Aurora was due to deliver her morning medications.

"Madam Reyna," Aurora called softly as she entered the room. With careful steps, she approached Reyna. In her hands she held a serving tray laden with an assortment of pills and herbal teas.

"Thank you, Aurora," Reyna murmured, offering a weak smile as she gingerly reached for a cup. "Your dedication never ceases to amaze me."

"It is no bother, Madam," Aurora replied. "I just wish I could do more to help you feel better."

Reyna regarded her maid thoughtfully.

"Aurora," she began, her voice laced with sympathy, "there is something I must tell you." She hesitated, searching for the right words to convey the truth without causing further distress.

Aurora's eyes widened with curiosity and worry. "Madam Reyna, is something wrong?"

Reyna took a deep breath. "Someone has been stealing from the company. It's been going on for some time now, but I have finally found out who it is and have referred the matter to the police. Oh, Aurora, I am so sorry, but it is your nephew, Alon."

Aurora's eyes widened and she gasped in shock. "Alon? No, it can't be. He is a good man."

"I'm afraid it's true. The evidence is overwhelming."

"But Madam, you could call off the police. Just fire him if you must, but please don't have him arrested. He has a family. This will ruin them!"

"I'm sorry, Aurora. It's out of my hands."

A heavy silence fell between them as Aurora walked over to the window and fixed her gaze on the outside garden. When she turned back to Reyna, her eyes were filled with rage.

"It's not that you can't. You won't. And for that, you'll pay!"

Aurora then stormed out of the room, leaving a stunned Reyna wondering what her normally even-tempered and kind employee could possibly have meant.

Filipino folklore is replete with stories of the Mangkukulam, practitioners of a kind of witchcraft known as kulam. Combining folk spirituality and healing with mysticism and sorcery, kulam is still practiced today in the Philippines by both young and old adherents. The Mangkukulam are known for their adeptness in spellcasting, the skill to cast curses, and their proficiency in various other occult practices. They are often described as individuals who wield their supernatural abilities for both good and evil purposes, depending on their intentions and the needs of those who come to them for help. In Filipino culture, these practitioners carry a complex reputation, evoking both apprehension and intrigue for their extraordinary powers.

It was to the house of a Mangkukulam that Aurora went after she angrily left Reyna Santos.

Appearing at the door to greet the upset maid was an attractive middle-aged woman dressed in a sky-blue tunic top and white linen pants. Her makeup was modest but flattering, and her perfume subtle but pleasant. Aurora wondered if this was indeed the Mangkukulam she had been directed to, as the woman before her was a far cry from the hideous old hag Aurora had been warned about as a child.

Sensing Aurora's uncertainty, the woman said, "I am the one you are looking for. Come in and tell me how I may help you."

Aurora followed the woman into the living room and then, taking a seat, began relating in a quiet voice the events that led her here. But as she continued talking, her words grew more vicious and her delivery of them more furious. Soon she was fully launched into a tirade about the "injustice" and "destruction" Reyna Santos was bringing upon her family, her anger swelling like a raging inferno. Aurora spat out her final words to the Mangkukulam in a voice that echoed through the room: "I want to see her suffer! I want to see her die!"

The Mangkukulam remained unmoving during Aurora's outburst. In the silence that followed, the woman reached for a notepad and scribbled something on it. She gave it to Aurora. "That is my price. If you agree to it, I will need something personal from your mistress, a hairbrush, for example. I also need you to know that the curse I will cast is immutable. I cannot call it back once it is sent."

Aurora nodded eagerly. "I will get what you need."

As she left the house of the Mangkukulam, Aurora felt almost giddy. Reyna will now get what she deserves!

As Aurora knew the Santos household schedule better than anyone, it was a simple matter of slipping into the house the next morning unseen and snatching Reyna's hairbrush from the bathroom vanity. The silver strands entangled in the teeth would soon be the last to fall from that woman's head, Aurora thought to herself as she tucked the brush in her purse and scampered quickly from the grounds.

That night, Aurora returned to the Mangkukulam and presented the filched brush. The woman, now dressed in a satiny black robe, carefully plucked several hairs from the brush and placed them on a silver tray. Then she sprinkled pungent oils over the strands while chanting in the old tongue that Aurora could only partially understand. When she was finished, she breathed heavily over the hairs three times, then turned to Aurora and said, "It is done."

Aurora spent the next several days in agonizing anticipation of news of her employer's sudden demise. But as the days trickled by without incident, Aurora couldn't help but wonder if the spell had failed. The witch had assured her it could not. So she waited again as patiently as possible.

After the seventh night had passed with no news, Aurora enlisted her cousin, a friend of Loy's, to visit the gardener and casually ask about Reyna's health. After all, maybe she was just deteriorating slowly (and painfully, Aurora hoped). But upon returning, her cousin reported, "The widow thrives. I saw her walking in the garden without even a sniffle."

Rage boiled in Aurora's blood. She marched to the Mangkukulam's house and pounded on the door. "Your magic did nothing! The widow still lives!"

The door flung open and the once-placid woman whom Aurora had dealt with before now stood before her shaking with anger. "You did not tell me the widow was one of *them*," she snarled. "She is protected, you fool."

Aurora frowned. Protected by whom?

The witch threw up her arms. "Your mistress is a true believer," explained the witch. "I found out from another that not only is she a regular churchgoer, but she attends the Charismatic Center downtown. Their priests cleanse curses and send back the spirits we cast."

Aurora had not given much thought to Reyna's religious life. She knew the widow was Catholic and did Catholic things, but not being a believer herself, she had not specifically discussed religion with Reyna. She just assumed it was a minor part of her employer's life, as it was for so many. Something done to keep up appearances. But now, seeing how upset the Mangkukulam was, a rising sense of fear gripped Aurora's heart.

"So what do we do?"

"*We* don't do anything. *I* will do what is necessary to protect myself. Now go! I am done with you!" And with that she slammed the door, leaving Aurora shaken and confused.

Understanding slowly started to seep into Aurora's brain. The curse was not only being repelled but likely reversing. If the witch herself was afraid of what might happen, how did she have any hope for herself?

She hurried home and locked herself in her bedroom. Perhaps Reyna would take her back, she thought. If the widow was truly protected from magic as the witch declared, then just being in her presence might be enough to be saved. No. Aurora shook her head. No, that's not enough. She would have to confess everything to Reyna and hope for forgiveness. Her anger and resentment. Her deal with the Mangkukulam. Her wish for Reyna to—

She collapsed on her bed and sobbed. How could she have let things get to this point?

As the hours passed, Aurora slipped restlessly in and out of sleep, her mind and body refusing her the solace she sought from slumber. She finally awakened fully, but it wasn't to the morning light as she had hoped. Rather, the darkest part of the night seemed to have settled in her room, along with an unsettling presence that caused the tiny hairs on her neck and arms to stand on end. She clutched at her blanket, trying to steady herself against the rising fear in her chest and the unnatural cold that suddenly filled the room. She listened for sounds of assurance—traffic speeding by, a television blaring, a siren wailing—but what she heard instead made her tremble even more. Floorboards creaking in cadence to phantom steps. Coming ever and ever closer.

Aurora closed her eyes tightly and pulled the blanket over her face, hoping to find refuge in a hidden corner of her mind. But the nightmare continued. Spectral figures materialized in her mind's eye. Ghostly shadows danced in a macabre ballet, intertwining and twirling around one another, as haunting whispers echoed through the corners of her consciousness.

When Aurora opened her eyes again, morning light happily greeted her. She blinked away the sleep that had finally come amid last night's theater of terror. She couldn't go through another night of that! Holding fast to her resolve to set things right, she jumped out of bed and quickly got dressed. She had to see Reyna. There was no time to waste.

As Aurora drove up the curving driveway to the Santos mansion, she looked appreciatively at the gardens that graced the estate. Loy was out pruning the bougainvillea, and Lita was out picking herbs for the day's meals. Everything seemed so normal, and for a moment Aurora felt hope that she could slide back into her old life. She parked the car and rehearsed in her mind what she would say to Reyna.

But as she looked out at the grounds that had just moments before filled her with lightness, she suddenly felt her equilibrium slip out from under her. In disbelief, she watched as the vibrant colors of the flowers turned a sickly gray and the familiar workers disappeared from sight, their places taken by pale, shapeless figures flickering behind palm trees, peering out from vine-knotted branches, and floating along the carabao grass. Aurora's heart dropped as she watched them move in her direction. She knew what they were here for. They had been promised a life. And they were here to collect.

As much as she wanted to run from the car into the house and throw herself at the feet of Reyna, begging forgiveness, she feared the faceless creatures more. Filled with despair, Aurora drove back home and readied herself for her inevitable fate. In one last act that she hoped would save someone else, if not herself, from the consequences of untethered rage, she wrote down the events that had brought her to this point. *May it serve as a warning,* she thought, as she stuffed the handwritten pages into an envelope she marked "Open Upon My Death." Then, she repeated the dictum of the Mangkukulam from weeks ago: "It is done."

At the funeral, mourners were heard repeating the same sentiments:

"Poor Aurora."

"Her death was so unexpected."

"Who knew her heart would give out without any warning?"

There was one woman who knew, though. She stood quietly behind a neighboring headstone, a respectable distance away from family and friends. Dressed fashionably in a black pantsuit and bearing a subtle yet pleasant scent, she felt neither sadness nor surprise. She had, after all, warned the woman being lowered into the ground.

A curse always finds a victim.

"The evil they wish on another will come back to them. A demon is never invoked in vain."

– Fr. Jose Antonio Fortea, exorcist and author

CHAPTER 4

New Age Deception

The modern New Age Movement can trace its roots back to the Theosophical Society founded by Russian-born Helena Petrovna Blavatsky in 1875 in New York. A resurgence of sorts began in the 1960s with the countercultural embrace of the occult, and it has steadily been growing ever since. Today, it has exploded into the mainstream with its hugely popular, wide umbrella of beliefs that blend the theology of pantheistic Eastern religions with practices from Western occultism. Promising personal empowerment, cosmic enlightenment, and esoteric knowledge, the New Age Movement is the perfect stomping ground for liars, deceivers, and thieves—especially those of the non-human variety.

* * *

Gina knew she was different at an early age. As a young child, she had a number of out-of-body experiences, which were most often triggered when something distressing happened to her. One such experience occurred at a playground when her parents, busy with ushering their tired and cranky other children into the car after a chaotic sporting event, inadvertently left her behind. They came screeching back fifteen minutes later, but in the meantime, Gina contentedly sat under the monkey bars in her body while her mind floated high above the play equipment, taking in the sea of bustling

43

children until she saw her family's minivan turn into the parking lot and speed over in her direction. Another time, she slipped down some icy stairs and broke her arm. As doctors attended to her in the ER, she watched their every action from over their heads and later asked her shocked—and blushing— nurse if it hurt when the doctor pinched her bottom.

When Gina was 12, she started having premonitions in her dreams about family members. In one dream, she saw her father smoking at her grandmother's funeral. When her grandmother unexpectedly died a few weeks later, her father, who hadn't had a cigarette in ten years, did indeed light up outside the funeral parlor.

Although her family identified nominally as Christian, Gina remembers more dinner table discussions about the paranormal, the occult, and Eastern mysticism than anything having to do with Jesus, prayer, and the Bible. In fact, Gina's great-aunt was a psychic and a self-proclaimed healer who had a great deal of influence on Gina. Suspecting that her grandniece shared her abilities, she took her to a tarot card reader for a formal assessment. Not surprisingly, the reader told Gina she had a gift and urged her to develop it. Gina was thrilled, as any young girl would be who had just been told she was special. She began making visits to the reader on a regular basis, not only to hear what the future held for her, but also to learn the craft and be able to tell others their futures.

As Gina matured into a self-assured, successful young woman, so did her psychic abilities grow in diversity and strength. At the recommendation of her tarot card mentor, she joined a divination group, where she fully immersed herself in channeling, meditation, automatic writing, and all facets of New Age practices and philosophies. She knew she had reached a higher level of proficiency when, one night, she had a dream about a deceased man she didn't know. She soon found out that the man in the dream was related to her ex-boyfriend's new girlfriend and that the information she received about this deceased person (that he had fathered a child outside his marriage) was spot-on. Gina was shocked because this was the first time she had received psychic information about someone who wasn't a friend or relative. It confirmed, in her mind, that it wasn't her subconscious picking up subtle clues about people; it was something else, something extra-sensory that she had either been born with or gifted with.

Confident in her newly-honed abilities, Gina began to do readings for people for a nominal fee. At first, she didn't want to charge anything, but was told by the other members of her divination group that she needed to, as it was a proper "exchange of energy." She also started teaching classes at the local New Age bookshop, offering courses in such diverse fares as past-life regression, clairvoyance, remote viewing, manifestation, and automatic writing.

Gina had a particular attachment to automatic writing, as it was the primary method by which she received information for her clients. In practice, "spirit" would move her hands to write out messages from deceased loved ones or to foretell future events. She neither had to look at what she was writing nor put any physical effort into her hands and arms. In essence, she conceded total control to a third-party, spiritual force. While some people would balk at letting themselves "be used" in such a way, Gina believed, like many of her psychic friends, that she genuinely was doing good deeds for others by bringing them in contact with their lost loved ones.

But as much as she outwardly projected goodness and light, Gina was experiencing increasingly frequent episodes of darkness. Depression and eating disorders ravished her mental and physical well-being. Voices that she previously heard in relation to other people's lives were more and more being directed at her in taunting and threatening ways: "You're worthless." "Who do you think you are?" "You can do nothing without us." And the most disturbing: "We're never letting you go."

Along with these continual bashings to her psyche, Gina was enduring physical attacks in her home. Pictures on her walls would suddenly drop as she walked by. Cabinet doors would fling open, missing hitting her in the face by mere inches. And something, or someone, would touch her randomly, sometimes while she was on the treadmill, in the shower, or at the top of a staircase. But the most frightening occurrences were the manifestations of what she could only describe at the time as "creatures." Some appeared as strange-looking animals, real in some ways and phantasmagoric in others. Some were simply shadows that assumed any number of different shapes and sizes, some human-looking and some monstrous. On several occasions, a Grim Reaper-type figure appeared in her hall, its face hidden behind the folds of a black hood.

While many would reach out to the nearest exorcist at this point, Gina still believed she could solve her problems on her own. She had learned from her New Age teachings that it was possible to filter out spirits, the good from the bad. Since she was obviously being plagued by negative or "bad" spirits, she resorted to using all the metaphysical means of protection that she knew of. She burned sage, used smudging sticks, hung crystals, and imagined white light surrounding her—nothing worked.

Up to this point, Gina's supernatural attacks had only happened in private, with Gina as the only witness. That changed one wintery day while she was giving a tarot card reading at her usual place of business, the back of the bookshop. Her client, a middle-aged woman who had been to Gina before, sat expectantly across the table, intent on the cards displayed before her and on Gina's explanation of their meaning. When Gina suddenly stopped talking in the middle of a sentence, the woman looked up and gasped in horror. Gina's attractive and normally placid face had been replaced by a grotesque and unrecognizable visage more akin to an animal than a human. The woman jumped back from her chair, nearly knocking over the table that held the cards. She continued to watch in amazement as Gina's face shimmied and morphed back and forth between beast and human, locked as it were in a struggle for dominance. Suddenly the vacillation stopped and Gina's face returned to normal, apart from the look of confusion at seeing her client's terrified expression.

That night, Gina sat alone in her house and thought about what to do next. For the first time in her life, she was unsure about the psychic path she had journeyed on for over two decades. Instead of feeling confident and in control, she felt afraid and disoriented. What was happening to her had all the earmarks of demonic oppression, yet she believed she had done nothing to invite such forces into her world. She had worked hard her whole life to keep negativity at bay for herself and her clients through the good and judicious use of her "gifts." So why now this harassment from hell? At her wits' end, she closed her eyes…and prayed.

Two days later, a friend invited Gina to her church. Not ready yet for that big of a step, Gina declined. But as the weeks went on and she fell further into depression and loneliness, she knew she had to try something different. She accompanied her friend to a service and felt a power course through her unlike any she had experienced in her psychic undertakings. Over the next few months, Gina threw herself into the study of Scripture and received pastoral counseling before finally coming to the conclusion that she had been duped by the New Age movement, despite being a most ardent devotee for over twenty years. As she now readily admits, her turnaround in thinking was a surprise to everyone, most of all herself.

"There is no such thing as a 'good spirit' that talks to a psychic," Gina tells people when asked about her former profession. "They're all demons playing a part. Some just dress up better than others." Active on the interview circuit, Gina uses her inside knowledge these days to try to steer people away from the occult and, particularly, to cast shade on an occultist's ability to foretell events. She explains that any accurate predictions that come from a fortune teller are in reality coming from demons, who use their advanced intelligence and eons of experience living alongside humans to posit likely outcomes of strings of actions.

Similarly, the phenomenon of "manifesting" via vision boards, affirmations, and lunar cycles is driven by demonic forces, she warns. Little more than a friendly form of witchcraft, Gina believes that these practices and their overarching principle, the Law of Attraction, are a plague on society, leading many spiritually vulnerable people "down a rabbit hole of destruction."

While non-relenting in her crusade against the New Age and occult practices, she also recognizes that not all practitioners are inherently wicked or evil. Many psychics and mediums believe their gift is from God and that they are using it for His purposes. Sadly, Gina says, most are being deceived. Their abilities come from the Master of Lies, who so often masquerades as an angel of light. On the other hand, there are some people with a genuine gift of sensitivity to the spiritual realm who can, for example, sense the presence of demons, departed souls, or even sometimes angels. These folks are often of great help in deliverance and exorcism ministries, and they will never ask for money or seek fame.

Though her resolve was strong and she had divine grace in her corner, Gina didn't have an easy time walking away from her former life. She continued to experience paranormal activities in her home, endured terrifying sleep paralysis episodes in bed, and even received unwanted "psychic" messages while sitting in church. While they still happen from time to time, the attacks have lessened the longer she has been away from her New Age lifestyle. The demons don't like to lose, she says, and so they will undoubtedly remind her of their presence from time to time.

Only now she knows she has nothing to fear. When the disquieting spirits come to harass her, instead of turning over a tarot card for guidance, she turns to a page in her Bible.

"Basically, when you're playing around with spirit communication, you're generally getting a demon that's going to pretend to be something that isn't scary. . . Once you lower your guard and you enter into that friendship, that relationship with them, then later it becomes controlling."

– Adam Blai, demonologist and exorcism expert

CHAPTER 5

The Love Spell From Hell

Selling itself as a "pre-Christian tradition" that promotes free thought, personal empowerment, and a connection with Mother Earth, it's not too surprising that witchcraft is one of the fastest-growing "religions" in the world. Even before the rise of the internet, access to occult books, spell accouterments, and other magical materials was easy to obtain from bookshops or mail-order businesses. Now, with internet access in nearly everyone's pocket via their phones, it's easier than ever to become a self-styled witch or warlock, or to hire one for spell-casting purposes. But whether the actions are learned from a book, as in the following story, or from a web page, the same danger remains: Once a shadowy force is summoned, it will spread its darkness over everyone in its path.

* * *

The flickering candles cast eerie shadows across Linda's face as she knelt before the makeshift altar, her black satin gown pooling around her like spilled ink. Her voice, timid at first, gained strength with each chanted word of the incantation.

"Hear my call, ye ancient powers who wield influence over mortal passions. Enflame the one whose name I have written in blood with unquenchable love and desire for me."

As she touched the blood-streaked paper to the candle flame, a clammy chill prickled her skin, sending shivers down her spine. The air grew heavy with an almost tangible sense of dread, and involuntarily, her gaze was drawn to the mirror at her side. Her eyes widened in horror, and had she not been paralyzed with fear, she would have screamed. For suddenly, she was not alone. A great, black mist with arm-like appendages loomed behind her reflection, its ominous presence leaning ever closer, threatening to suffocate the breath from her lungs.

Anguished sobs tore free from Linda's throat as the mist enveloped her, its tendrils snaking around her trembling form with a sinister grace. She squeezed her eyes shut, every muscle in her body rigid with terror, as the darkness seeped into her very essence, laying claim to its sacrificial host. Her mind raced, grasping at the fragments of her fading consciousness, but it was too late. The shadow had taken hold, its chilling embrace binding her fate to an ancient and malevolent force.

Linda had been adopted as a young child by an affluent New York family. Though she could have any material good she desired, what she really wanted was something money couldn't buy. She had become enamored with a motorcycle gang member named Jack, who was her antithesis in nearly every respect. She desperately attempted everything within her power to capture his attention, yet he hardly seemed to notice. The more her efforts were rebuffed, the more her obsession with him grew, until a friend kiddingly suggested casting a spell over Jack.

At first, Linda took the suggestion as the joke it was intended to be. But the idea never completely went away. It gnawed at her until she finally went to a bookstore and found several volumes on witchcraft. The books she chose had nothing to do, in her mind, with the darker arts of black magic or satanism. She was simply interested in entreating the spirits of love for assistance.

With that seemingly innocent purpose in mind, Linda performed the love-seeking ritual and reluctantly but willingly endured the embrace of the dark master she had invoked. As dreadful as that experience had been, Linda was delighted that a few days later Jack responded to her advances. The spell worked! But as the year went on, it became apparent that the cost of its success was higher than she could ever have imagined. Higher, even, than what a relationship with Jack was worth.

The night of the ritual was the entity's first of many manifestations. It frequently appeared in the evenings when Linda was home alone, lingering as a shadow in the periphery of her vision. Sometimes it would awaken her in bed, crushing her with its weight upon her chest and paralyzing her with such fear that she couldn't yell out. Even when she couldn't see it, she could sense its presence, feeling its cold, hideous touch or hearing its telepathic whispers.

"You belong to me, Linda. You are mine! Recall your vow, Linda? You promised to do anything for me if I made Jack fall for you. Well, Jack does love you, Linda. Jack truly loves you!"

Only after obtaining Jack's affection did Linda realize her mistake. Her dream lover was cruel and controlling, and now she found herself trapped in a Faustian nightmare. No matter how hard she tried to rid herself of Jack, the entity wouldn't allow it. Whenever she attempted, its attacks on her would intensify. She would find herself compelled to do things against her will. It forced her to hurt her loved ones. It made her shout at them and say things she would never normally say. It encouraged her to commit any wrongdoing she desired, assuring her that no one would ever find out. The more Linda fought against the audacious suggestions it put in her head or whispered in her ear, the more relentless it was in its efforts to break her will.

More often than not, she gave in. She continued to immerse herself in witchcraft, but the seemingly harmless "white" magic she had started with was now left behind, replaced by black magic rituals to exalt and summon the demonic. As much as one part of her struggled to resist these practices, a weaker part fell prey to the siren call of her nefarious dark lord, and she would hear her own voice answering, "Heed me, for I am yours … Your meek servant, your daughter, Linda…"

A year of terror and near-psychological enslavement ensued before Linda, then age 19, confided in a close college friend by the name of Pete. As Linda confessed everything to him—the obsession with Jack, the witchcraft rituals, and the horrific consequences she was now enduring—Pete recalled a seminar given on campus by a paranormal investigator and demonologist. What Linda was telling him seemed to be right in presenter John Murphy's area of expertise. Without too much urging, Linda agreed to meet with him.

"What does it say it wants, Linda?" asked the robust man sitting across the table from her.

Linda stared at the coffee cup between her hands and remained silent for several moments. She had shared most of her story with John Murphy and was grateful for his non-judgmental manner. But she didn't know if she could answer this particular question. It wasn't that she didn't know the answer. She did, oh, she did…

"Linda?" John gently prodded.

"It says it's going to rip out my heart for meeting with you, and then send me to the sea of oblivion for all eternity. It's going to rip out my tongue and pluck out my eyes." She looked up at John with tears streaming down her face.

"Oh, please help me! I swear, I didn't know what I was doing. I never intended to be a devil worshiper. I just thought I was doing a harmless little love spell. But now I'm being forced to do these…these despicable things." She paused, catching her breath. "It gets worse. It wants me to kill Pete. And I'm afraid it'll force me and I won't be able to resist!"

John did his best to encourage Linda not to give up, nor, of course, to give in. He had seen many young people get entangled in the web of the occult, and he had seen many escape. As he told her, good will always win over evil. She just needed to be open to it. He then asked her if she was ready to renounce her ties to witchcraft and any and all allegiance to the Evil One. She answered vehemently that she was.

As Pete held her hand, John then conducted an exorcism ritual over Linda. When he was done, Linda felt a sense of peace unlike anything she could remember. That night, when she went to bed in John's guest room, she fell asleep finally unafraid of the dark hours ahead. It was a small victory, but one of many she hoped were on their way.

The following morning, Linda and Pete departed John's residence to return to their college in upstate New York. The drive started out positive. Linda was filled with determination to combat the demon that was trying to destroy her. For even though John Murphy had driven it away last night, she was not naive enough to think it was gone for good. Her plan of action would start with giving up Jack, no matter what obstacles were thrown at her. Unfortunately, those obstacles came sooner than expected.

A few hours into the drive, Linda experienced a new phenomenon for the first time, a sharp pain across her chest, making breathing extremely difficult. The pain persisted for several agonizing minutes before subsiding. Twice more that day, she felt the same pain. It was entirely unlike anything she had ever experienced before. She was terrified. She thought perhaps she had developed a tumor or some other equally serious condition.

That night, the demon came to her again. She could sense the black cloud next to her bed, hear the whispered seductions in her head. With every fiber of her being, she resisted its attack by loudly renouncing its power over her and saying the prayers John had suggested until, finally, it left.

Over the next few weeks, the mysterious pain continued to come and go. Doctors couldn't give her an answer as to what was causing it, leaving Linda to form her own theory, namely, that it was not of this world. Her suspicions were confirmed when she suddenly began experiencing an overwhelming desire to quit school, go back to Jack, and return to Satanism. When she tried to banish these thoughts from her head, the pain would intensify. Even more distressing, the urge to kill Pete kept entering her mind, along with the compelling thought that by killing Pete, she would kill the pain. But Linda's resolve proved stronger than the demon's snare, and finally, after putting up a spirited resistance for a month that seemed more like a year, the hellish torture began to subside.

For a while, Linda's world appeared normal. Her classes were going well, Jack had faded from her life, and the demonic assaults had ceased. Overall, a sense of purpose and peace accompanied her most days. Then, during an English class, she was given an assignment to write about a subject she knew a lot about. Of course, witchcraft and Satanism came immediately to mind. The Friday night before the paper was due, Linda encountered a peculiar dream in which the demon attempted to reconnect with her. She awoke, only to find that the nightmare was real. The entity that had terrorized her for so long was back, lurking in her room as an impenetrable black mass. It beckoned to her, urging her to join it. Once again, Linda resisted, focusing on positive imagery and her new-found allegiance to the Divine Good. Her efforts were successful and the entity vanished.

The next evening, Linda, Pete, her brother, and some other acquaintances were seated at the campus cafeteria when the intense chest pain she had experienced a few weeks prior struck again.

"It felt like someone was stepping on my chest, preventing my lungs from inflating," she recalled. "I could barely breathe!"

She then lost consciousness, but her eyes remained wide open in horror. As the helpless onlookers watched, Linda's body began to jerk wildly in her chair, pushing the table away and knocking various items to the floor. After several minutes, the bucking stopped and Linda awoke, nauseous and pale. She had no recollection of the experience except what her friends reported.

The following day, Sunday, she felt like she was going to pass out again and went to the hospital. The physician there stated that her heart was fine, as were all her other bodily functions. It was likely just a minor seizure, he told her, and then advised her that if the incident did not reoccur, there was no need for concern. It could have been caused by stress or any number of factors. Linda, however, was not satisfied with that explanation. She wanted assurance that it would not happen again.

On Monday, Linda visited the school infirmary, where they referred her to a Syracuse hospital for an electro-cardiogram. She underwent every conceivable test in an attempt to uncover the cause of her "seizure." The results of all the tests fell within normal parameters, and epilepsy was also ruled out. She was prescribed tranquilizers and once again informed that if the seizure did not reoccur, she should not be concerned.

But as Linda soon found out, there was still reason to be concerned. Thursday morning, she awoke feeling unwell once more. She also realized that her body was involuntarily jerking about on the bed—the same type of seizure she had in the cafeteria, but this time she was conscious. A terrible pain arose in her chest, and black spots circled before her eyes. She lay in bed for more than an hour, not only enduring the physical torments on her body but also formulating in her mind the remedy doctors could not provide her.

As soon as the assault let up—for she had no doubts now as to the demonic origin of her maladies—Linda set to work destroying all of her ritualistic paraphernalia, books, art, and anything else remotely connected to the occult, including the notes for her English essay. The realization came to her that morning that, while she was sincere at the time of her exorcism in renouncing her ties to witchcraft and satanism, she hadn't flushed out every trace of attachment. A small part of her wanted those tangibles there "just in case." But no more, she vowed, as she burned or threw away every last piece of satanic trappings.

Linda's concerted efforts to never again engage in occult practices proved successful this time. The physical assaults subsided, although from time to time she still experienced the urge to harm Pete. During those episodes, if she was with Pete, she forced herself to walk away from him as quickly as possible. There were also a few times when she would wake up in the middle of the night and sense the demon's presence in the room with her. Over time, she found it easier and easier to resist the whispered temptations, resorting to positive imagery and prayer to drive the foul entity away. Eventually, the demon's visits stopped completely.

It had a new target in its sights.

Throughout Linda's ordeal, Pete had been apprehensive of demonic retribution. After all, he was the one who insisted that Linda seek assistance from John Murphy and who was there supporting her at every step of her lifestyle change. It was he, in effect, who took Linda from the entity's reach. Unfortunately, in so doing, he put himself within it.

A few months after Linda had achieved final freedom from the demon, Pete began experiencing terrifying nightmares in which a voice demanded that he stab his parents to death. As the dreams progressed in intensity, Pete watched himself succumbing to the dark commands and viciously killing his mother and father with a kitchen knife. He also began having daytime fantasies and urges to hurt unsuspecting strangers that he passed on the street, as well as friends and colleagues. The compulsion to inflict pain quickly escalated into an all-consuming desire to kill. Fearing for the safety of those around him, Pete made the heart-wrenching decision to move to the West Coast, as far away as possible from everyone he knew and loved.

Before his departure, Pete had confided in Linda about the demonic attacks. But after several months in his self-imposed exile, he abruptly ceased all contact with her, leaving his fate a distressing mystery. Despite the unsettling silence, Linda continued to hope that Pete was able to somehow, somewhere, find the strength needed to battle his oppressor. She knew all too well from her own experience that he would need such strength in great abundance to have any chance of prevailing.

For Linda understood with grim certainty an undeniable truth about the demonic: it hated to lose.

> *"The next thing that I knew, I was seeing things, hearing things, and I was being tortured by demonic spirits that had come in through the use of witchcraft. It was a very scary time. I didn't even want to close my eyes to wash my face. I was that terrified. If you think that it is innocent, I am telling you it will take you down a road you do not want to go down."*
>
> **– Jenny Weaver, former witch**

CHAPTER 6

The Devil's Concerto

Selling one's soul to the devil is a concept that dates back to antiquity but was perhaps best immortalized by the legend of Faust, a scholar who makes a pact with the devil, offering his soul in exchange for knowledge, power, and worldly pleasures. The term "Faustian bargain" has since transcended its literary origins to symbolize any agreement where short-term benefits are obtained at the expense of long-term consequences, particularly when it involves ethically dubious actions or compromises. But according to many exorcists, these devilish deals can and do occur outside the figurative realm, with often unfortunate and harrowing results.

* * *

Sarah tucked a loose strand of hair behind her ear as she lifted her violin to her chin. The stage lights beat down on her, highlighting the sheen of sweat on her forehead. She took a deep breath and closed her eyes, letting the first notes of her solo ring out into the concert hall.

The melody soared through the air, resonating with a haunting beauty. Sarah's bow danced across the strings, coaxing out the bittersweet lament of the solo. She poured her heart into the music, expressing all the sorrow and longing inside her.

Too soon, the final notes faded away, leaving a ringing silence. The applause startled Sarah out of her reverie. She blinked at the bright lights, the spell broken. As she bowed, she wondered if this audition would be the final one. Since graduating from Juilliard, she had been to so many that she had lost count. At each one, she had performed flawlessly, only to receive empty accolades while her peers received job offers with major orchestras and chamber groups.

She began packing up her instrument and music sheets when the conductor came over, thanked her for playing, and then, in a practiced apologetic voice, told her they had decided on someone else but to feel free to audition again if a position opened up. Sarah had heard these familiar words so often she could have recited them in sync with him.

After he and the other committee members left the hall, Sarah slumped down on the edge of the empty stage, staring at the floor. She had poured everything into that performance, but it hadn't been enough. Everyone was moving on to orchestras and solo careers, while she was still stuck here. Hot tears pricked at her eyes.

"I would give anything to be famous," she whispered. "Anything."

Clutching her violin case like a talisman, Sarah headed toward the exit. Immersed in her own dark mood, she barely noticed that the lights in the cavernous hall had nearly all turned off. A sudden icy shudder went through her and she stopped short. She turned, sensing someone behind her, but all she saw were ominous and encroaching shadows. She took a stumbling step back, and then quickly made her way out of the building.

Sarah tossed and turned that night, unable to sleep. The applause for her solo still rang in her ears even as the sting of rejection burned in her brain. After fits and starts, she finally drifted off, but into a strange and disturbing dream world. She found herself walking down a narrow corridor, the walls and floor made of rough stone. Up ahead, a door stood ajar, candlelight flickering through the crack. Sarah drifted toward it as if compelled. She pushed the door open and froze.

The room was sumptuously decorated with velvet drapes and gilded furniture. In the center was an ornate throne, upon which sat a strikingly handsome, naked young man. He gazed at Sarah with an intensity that pinned her in place.

"Hello, my dear. I've been waiting for you."

Sarah's mouth went dry. She knew she should flee, but her feet carried her forward until she stood an arm's length away from him, trembling. The man stared at her with hypnotic eyes.

"You wish to be famous, do you?" His words wove through her mind like silk. "I can make that happen."

Sarah swayed, her thoughts growing murky. "Yes," she heard herself say. "More than anything."

The man snapped his fingers and into his perfectly manicured hand appeared a piece of parchment paper and an old-fashioned quill pen.

"Sign this paper with your blood and fame shall be yours."

Sarah took the paper with trembling hands. She pricked her thumb on the quill's sharp nib, staining the parchment crimson as she signed her name. The man locked eyes with her, his gaze hypnotic and never wavering even as he took back the contract and added his own sanguine signature.

Sarah broke free of his stare and tried to decipher the cryptic scrawl beside hers, but soon it didn't matter, as the moving threads of viscous red mingled into an unreadable blur. Then the man blew gently, and the parchment burst into flames, its edges curling and blackening before turning to a fine mist of ash that drifted softly to the floor.

Sarah awoke with a gasp, her heart pounding and sweat soaking her face and chest. Just a dream, she told herself, laughing nervously at the bizarre details she could recall so clearly. Glancing down, she was shocked to see a small cut on her finger and traces of ash on her sheets. What the–? Shaken, she quickly cleaned herself up and resolved not to tell a soul about the strange dream or its aftereffects. Things were stressful enough right now and she didn't need anyone spreading rumors that she was crazy. The dream was crazy, for sure, but stress can manifest strange things. That's what she told herself, at any rate, while ignoring the lingering unease in her heart.

In the coming weeks, Sarah forgot all about the strange dream as her life took an abrupt turn. Out of the blue, she received an invitation to audition for a world-renowned conductor. To her surprise and delight, three days later he offered her a coveted spot on an upcoming world tour.

As Sarah took the stage night after night in sold-out concert halls spanning the globe, the thunderous applause and standing ovations were almost too much to comprehend. Her years of diligent practice and perseverance through adversity had finally paid off in the sweetest of ways. From Paris to Prague, Tokyo to Sydney, Sarah captivated audiences with her virtuosic playing and heartfelt musicality.

Backstage, fans clamored for her autograph and praised her flawless technique and emotional expressiveness. Glowing reviews in prestigious publications marveled at her prodigious talent and predicted a meteoric rise to stardom. Sarah could hardly believe that her childhood dream of becoming a famous musician was now her reality. The long hours, financial struggles, and family sacrifices had all been vindicated. Still, feelings of inadequacy and doubts nagged at her, as well as the unbidden thought that she had not yet paid her dues. When she had these broodings, a vague image of a strange man teased at her memory but dissipated like dust before fully materializing.

Caught up in the thrill of celebrity, Sarah embraced the rock star lifestyle for many years. Late nights, parties filled with celebrities and fans, and excessive alcohol became the norm for her. She also began experimenting with recreational drugs, sparingly at first, but eventually she developed a dangerous dependence on cocaine to artificially boost her energy to get through her demanding performance schedule.

As one particularly grueling tour progressed, Sarah grew increasingly paranoid, anxious, and isolated. She saw strange shadows lurking in the corners of whatever room she was in, and she couldn't shake the feeling that someone was always watching her. Though she had told herself she would never do any "hard drugs," her deteriorating mental state broke down her resolve, and she eventually resorted to heroin to ease her growing performance anxiety before going on stage each night. Sarah knew deep down that her new vices were destructive, but she felt unable to pull herself out of the downward spiral.

Before long, Sarah had become a full-blown addict. Though she tried to hide it, her playing suffered noticeably, and soon rumors swirled as to whether or not she would even make it on stage. Then came a crippling blow. The conductor who had initially championed Sarah made it clear he would not work with her again.

Sarah's once-promising career took a sharp nosedive in the months that followed. Deep in the throes of addiction, she became increasingly unreliable, sometimes unable to even hold her violin bow properly due to uncontrollable withdrawal tremors. Word traveled quickly in the tight-knit orchestral community as to Sarah's condition, and almost overnight, the prestigious performance opportunities that once came so easily now completely dried up.

Her career wasn't the only thing in jeopardy at this point. Her careless use of street drugs resulted in her contracting HIV. How long she had the virus she wasn't sure, but it had been in her body long enough to severely compromise her immune system, and one bleak winter day she found herself in a New York City hospital with a deadly AIDS-related infection.

As she lay desperately ill, her past came rushing back. Sarah now remembered the strange dream from years ago and the contract signed in blood. Had she actually made some sort of pact with Satan? She wondered if all the professional success she had achieved had only been part of an infernal bargain that was now coming due. Facing death, Sarah feared that she had condemned herself to damnation.

Not knowing where else to turn, Sarah reached out to her estranged mother, a devout Catholic, and confessed everything: her wild lifestyle, her drug use, her current illness—and her suspected deal with the devil. Her mother didn't need to hear anymore. She immediately contacted the diocesan chancery and begged for an exorcist to be sent to her daughter's bedside.

The archbishop responded swiftly, assigning the task to Father James LeBlanc, a priest with extensive experience in conducting exorcisms. He arrived at the hospital and listened solemnly to Sarah's anguish-laden confession. Though he neither admonished nor blamed Sarah for her current situation, he did nonetheless make clear that she was under demonic influence and that she would have to "fight fire with fire." He then asked her if she was ready to renew her commitment to Christ. Without hesitation, she said yes. Then he told her she must write out the words of the Apostle's Creed, cut her finger, and sign the paper with her blood. In other words, she must reverse the pact.

Although Sarah was ready to do anything at this point to save her soul, the medical personnel in the room were adamantly not on board. The last thing they wanted a patient with HIV to do was bleed out among non-infected people. Plus, given Sarah's extremely compromised immune system, any cut could turn septic and kill her. While the doctors and Father LeBlanc argued back and forth on how to proceed, Sarah busied herself with writing out the words of the Creed, a prayer she was surprised to discover she still remembered from her youth. With an overwhelming desire to reaffirm her faith and "seal the deal," she quietly pricked her finger and signed the paper with her blood.

At the very moment the last red droplet punctuated the page, Sarah's body was seized by convulsions. Alarms blared as she frantically thrashed and screamed in agony. Then, just as suddenly, she went silent and still. The room descended into chaos as doctors and nurses rushed to revive her and as her mother wailed in anguish. "This is all your fault!" she screamed at Father LeBlanc. "You killed my daughter!" The priest, his face pale with shock, could only stand there, his hands clasped together in silent prayer.

After what felt like an eternity, the monitors suddenly beeped to life. Everyone present held their breath as Sarah, who just moments before had been at death's edge, if not over, sat up abruptly in her hospital bed. Her eyes were wide open, and there was a look of pure elation on her face. "It's all gone!" she exclaimed, her voice filled with relief and joy. "I'm not sick anymore!" The doctors were stunned not only by her remarkable resuscitation but even more so by her adamancy that she was free from any infection. They had to admit that she certainly looked better. They quickly conducted a series of tests that confirmed the impossible: There was no trace of AIDS, HIV, or any other sickness in Sarah's body. All of it had simply, inexplicably, vanished.

From that day forward, Sarah devoted her life and talent to serving God and others, forever grateful for the second chance she had been given. She continued performing at private venues and community events, all the while discovering a new passion for teaching violin to young students. No longer driven by a desire for fame, Sarah found herself guided by a deeper sense of purpose and the peace that accompanied it.

"There are more than a few people in today's society who do make contracts with Satan, often unwittingly....In any contract with the Evil One, all the recipient ends up receiving is misery and death."

**– Msgr. Stephen Rossetti, exorcist for the
Archdiocese of Washington**

CHAPTER 7

Demons of Enlightenment

Esoteric practices have long fascinated those seeking deeper spiritual understanding and personal growth. From ancient mystical traditions to modern New Age philosophies, these belief systems promise enlightenment, self-realization, and access to hidden truths. However, as the following account illustrates, trusting in these methods to find inner peace, or to unlock mysteries that are not ours to understand, can lead to unexpected and potentially dangerous consequences. Just as the name Lucifer means "light bearer," not everything that appears bright and beautiful is what it seems.

* * *

Cory was a senior in high school when he had his first exposure to the occult. His girlfriend at the time had recently played with a Ouija board at a party, and she was so enthralled by it that she bought her own board and persuaded Cory to try it out with her. The couple's excitement soon dimmed, however, when their earnestly asked questions received no answers from the apparently indifferent spirit world. They were about to put the game away when suddenly, as Cory put it, "that thing in the middle just zoomed around on its own accord." The "thing" Cory referred to, of course, was the planchette, a small heart-shaped object designed to move under the fingertips of the players and point to the letters on the board in response to questions. While in some cases, players either intentionally or unintentionally "guide" the planchette, in this case, Cory was adamant that neither he nor his girlfriend moved it. In fact, their fingers weren't even on it when it spun around the board.

Cory was still thinking about the Ouija board session when, a few days later, his girlfriend's father, to whom Cory had grown close, became seriously ill and died unexpectedly. With so many unexplained questions now on his mind, and feeling like something major was missing from his life, Cory set out on a spiritual quest to find out more about the seen and the unseen world around him. The first stop on his journey came soon afterward when he saw an ad in a magazine declaring "Learn the Mysteries of Life!" The ad was from the Rosicrucians, also known as the Ancient and Mystical Order Rosae Crucis (Latin for "Rose Cross"), whose teachings date back to the early 17th century. Rosicrucian teachings are a mix of occultism and other religious beliefs and practices, including Hermeticism, Jewish mysticism, and early Christian Gnosticism. A central belief of the group is that each individual possesses a divine spark or inner divinity, and that through spiritual practices and self-discovery, one can realize and manifest this divine potential.

Captivated by this promise of ancient wisdom and exalted powers, Cory sent away for the Rosicrucian initiation kit and began a six-week period of study. After completing the "first-degree" coursework, he was directed to formally initiate himself into the order by performing a secret ceremony—a ritual of crystallomancy, or mirror divination, a practice dating back to the Greek and Roman oracles. Following the given instructions, Cory surrounded himself with lighted candles in a darkened room and stared into a mirror. Then he traced a five-inch cross on the glass while chanting, "Hail, holy cross," and concluded the rite with three minutes of meditation.

Having finished his initiation ritual, Cory turned his lights back on, blew out the candles, and settled down to do his math homework. As he flipped the pages of his textbook, he wondered if he would soon see any effects from his journey into mysticism, like maybe making his math problems easier to solve, he thought, chuckling to himself. He didn't have to wait long for an answer. As he hovered his pencil over his paper, an incredible sensation of hypersensitivity suddenly shot through him as if he'd been injected with a drug. He was looking at his paper, but seeing *through* it, seeing every infinitesimal element that made it up. He looked around his room and experienced the same hypersensitivity with everything he focused on. He was no longer looking *at* things but somehow *participating in* them.

A million questions bombarded his mind while he struggled with his altered consciousness. Questions like, "How does matter exist?" "Is what we see even real?" "Is there a God?" "Are *we* God?" Cory later recalled that what upset him the most about these questions was the feeling that they weren't coming from him but rather from some outside source. It was as if he was being programmed like a computer, and the longer it went on, the more he lost his feeling of "self."

Eventually, Cory's consciousness returned to normal, he finished his math, and he went on to finish high school. Throughout the years that followed, however, in college and at work, Cory couldn't help but feel that something had settled in him ever since that night of the Rosicrucian ritual—something alien. While he didn't experience that exact same metaphysical episode again that he had in his bedroom, he did have recurring bouts of cloudy thinking and feeling separated from his own being.

In an attempt to reclaim his inner peace, when he was in his mid-20s, Cory took up a friend's suggestion to try Transcendental Meditation (TM). Developed by Maharishi Mahesh Yogi in the mid-1950s, TM is a self-guided meditation practice where one silently repeats a mantra for 15-20 minutes. Its adherents claim it promotes relaxed awareness, stress relief, self-development, and higher states of consciousness. For Cory, it did all that and more. After a few months of practicing the method, he had another extraordinary experience. His consciousness again transformed, but this time in a seemingly positive way. All the negative feelings he had been carrying around for the past few years instantly melted away, and he was filled with joy and peace.

Excited by this new development, Cory delved deeper into TM and signed up for an advanced course, the TM-Sidhi program. Whereas regular TM strives to settle the active mind, Sidhi reactivates that settled mind and utilizes it in ways, through extended meditation and more focused mantras, that allow the devotee to gain mastery over the Natural Law. One popular Sidhi technique is "yogic flying," during which the body spontaneously lifts off the ground, "bringing waves of energy, exhilaration, and bliss," according to one TM website. This was the Sidhi technique Cory decided to concentrate on. For the first couple of weeks during his practice, nothing unusual happened. But then he began to feel something like electricity enter his spine, making him feel light and energetic.

So light, in fact, he claimed that while sitting in the lotus position he levitated off the floor. That, of course, was surprising in and of itself, but along with this infusion of body-lifting energy came an explosion of non-intelligible words from his mouth. Cory was delighted with the levitation, but not so much with the babble. He sought the advice of his TM teachers, who told him he had risen to a higher plane of consciousness and that the nonsensical words were just a sign of stress leaving the body.

As Cory's journey into the metaphysical was reaching new heights, so was his career as a musician. He was about to perform in his first concert as a pianist when he was introduced to yet another bit of esotericism by a friend who was an avid occultist. This friend gave Cory a gift to mark the happy occasion: an egg-shaped green crystal with the outline of an eye sketched on it. The crystal, the friend told Cory, would protect him from negative energies, attract good luck, and bring insight and mental clarity. Cory was delighted with the beautiful talisman. He rubbed his fingers over it every day and visualized all the positive attributes it would soon supposedly impart. He was therefore distraught when the exact opposite happened. Shortly after receiving the crystal, Cory began experiencing the same terrifying feelings he'd had in high school—doubts about reality, fear of the unknown, and alienation from himself—but much more intense. His mind was in turmoil, flooded with bizarre, unwanted thoughts that he thought had been banished for good with his regular TM practice. Recalling that time, Cory described it as if something was trying to pluck the very soul out of him.

Confused and scared, Cory reached out for help from a faith-based paranormal investigator. A lapsed Catholic but still a believer in God, Cory decided to go back to his roots to try to quell the spiritual and mental unrest that had seized him for the better part of a decade. After asking around, he was referred to a former police officer who was known for his expertise in investigating cases of demonic activity and for his success in helping people overcome such harassment.

The investigator, Ralph Sarchie, on whose work the 2014 movie *Deliver Us from Evil* was based, knew immediately upon meeting Cory that the young pianist was in trouble. "I detected a peculiar aura around Cory's head: a ring of yellow studded with ominous black dots," Ralph recalled. In addition to the strange aura, Ralph was also struck by the eerie atmosphere of Cory's home. It was something he recognized from many previous cases—cases involving the demonic. Ralph listened carefully as Cory talked about his experiences with Eastern mysticism and New Age practices, the temporary solutions they had provided in the past, and the growing confusion, agitation, and despair that were now taking hold.

As Cory spoke, Ralph knew with growing certainty that this was a classic case of occult involvement leading to a demonic attachment. The demon had taken over so thoroughly over such an extended period of time that Cory could no longer distinguish between his own consciousness and that of the evil spirit. Ralph received further evidence of the demon's occupancy when Cory told him about a disturbing experience he recently had at a Catholic healing Mass. During the service, Cory said that he felt extremely anxious and disjointed, as if an alien presence were taking over his body. Suddenly his head began reeling back and forth, and he heard himself shout out nonsensically,

"Nayacota!" over and over, much to the surprise of the gathered congregation. "I knew I was saying 'no,' and I knew it was because something in me was provoked," he explained.

Ralph tried explaining to Cory that he was demonically possessed, but Cory was not yet ready to accept such a dramatic assertion. "Are you sure?" he kept asking Ralph. Couldn't it just be "bad energy" or something psychological? His religious upbringing never touched on such subjects. In fact, at one church he attended, he was told the devil didn't exist. In the hope of bringing some immediate relief to the young musician, and perhaps some needed proof, Ralph asked if he could pray a series of deliverance prayers over him. Cory agreed. But like at the healing Mass, Ralph's prayers brought forth a swift and violent reaction. Cory began thrashing back and forth, grimacing and whimpering as if Ralph's words were burning his skin. When Ralph held up a crucifix, Cory shrieked in pain, then yelled out once again, "Nayacota! Nayacota!" At this point, Ralph ended the prayer session with a forceful "Amen," fearful that continuing would provoke the demon more than he was equipped to handle.

Once Cory seemed to return to his normal self, Ralph again tried to explain how there was a demonic spirit inside him and how it was making it impossible for Cory to sit through a religious service, as at the healing Mass, or to even sit peacefully during a prayer session. As to how the entity got there in the first place, Ralph explained that it was likely a combination of occult activities going back to Cory's teenage years, compounded by his involvement in TM. The problem with TM, Ralph explained, is that it ignores God and focuses solely on the "self." For someone like Cory, who had previously attracted the attention of dark forces via the occult, his practice of TM and its exhortation to clear the mind of all thoughts only made it easier for demonic spirits to "fill" that void, disguising themselves as alternate spiritual concepts. However, instead of bringing peace and self-realization, they ultimately bring chaos and confusion, destruction and despair.

Ralph sensed that Cory was beginning to understand and accept this explanation as to what was happening to him, and so he then asked Cory if he'd be willing to undergo an exorcism. Cory immediately said yes, and a date was set. As Ralph was packing up his interview equipment, which included a video camera, Cory mentioned one other unusual thing that had been plaguing him. He told Ralph that he didn't see things the way other people did. When Ralph asked him to clarify what he meant, he said, "I see things as if I have a veil over my eyes." Ralph found the remark interesting and a little mysterious, but it wasn't until the next day that he found out exactly what Cory meant.

Ralph was reviewing the film from the interview the following afternoon when he noticed round, transparent balls, or "spirit energy," moving around Cory at pronounced speed. Unlike spirit energy orbs from light or "good" sources, which are octagonal, these round orbs Ralph had seen before in homes infested with satanic spirits. He asked a colleague, Brother Andrew, a gifted psychic and religious brother with the St. Paul Society on Staten Island, to review the film for a second opinion, being careful not to say anything in advance that might bias the assessment. Not only did Brother Andrew see the same sinister orbs, but he also declared very matter-of-factly that the man in the film was possessed by a demon. Then he noted something else peculiar. He couldn't clearly see the man's face, he said, because it was "hidden under some kind of veil."

A week later, Cory arrived at Our Lady of the Rosary chapel, where Ralph and three muscular men were waiting to assist Bishop Robert McKenna with the scheduled exorcism. Bishop McKenna, a renowned exorcist of the Orthodox Roman Catholic Movement (not to be confused with mainstream Catholicism), began the ancient rite by seating Cory in a chair and giving him a crucifix to hold. Then he began reading aloud from the Roman Ritual, one of the official liturgical books of the Church. After an extended period of no reaction on Cory's part (as Ralph noted, it's often a struggle to get the demon to reveal itself), the bishop stopped reading and asked Cory how he felt. The musician replied that he was beginning to feel pain at the base of his spine. Bishop McKenna glanced at Ralph. Both men knew this was a major chakra point and most likely, based on Cory's information, the area where the demon had initially entered him.

Bishop McKenna immediately went on the offensive. "Tell me your name, demon!" he commanded. Cory remained silent. The bishop repeated the command. This time, Cory's head jerked back and a guttural sound came from his mouth. Bishop McKenna draped his stole around Cory's neck. Then he touched a blessed relic to Cory's forehead, chest, left shoulder, and right shoulder, in effect tracing the Sign of the Cross over him. Cory screamed out a vulgarity with such vehemence that it took those assisting by surprise. Bishop McKenna, however, was undeterred. In a strong voice, he continued intoning the words of the ritual while the demon roared back in ancient and unknown languages. Every so often it would yell out "Nayacota," the nonsense word for "no" it had uttered previously.

"Tell me your name!" the bishop once again commanded. Cory spat out an incomprehensible two-syllable word.

"How many are you?"

Receiving no response, Bishop McKenna sprinkled holy water on the musician. Cory yelled out another obscenity and then broke down with deep-throated sobs. As heart-wrenching as the sobs were, Ralph knew the demon was a liar and master manipulator, and he refused to meet the pleading eyes of his hostage. Bishop McKenna paid no mind to the cursing, crying, flailing man before him, but steadfastly continued the recitation of the exorcism rite. For two hours, the battle raged on. At times, Cory seemed in control, sitting calmly and seemingly thankful for the prayers and relics used on him. At other times, the demon was clearly taking over, recoiling from the blessed objects, jerking Cory's body around like a rag doll, and emitting snarls and shouts from the young man's abused mouth.

By the time Bishop McKenna was on the third reading of the ritual, Cory's yelling and jerking had subsided. In a small, feeble voice, he said that his back was in great pain. Ralph moved closer and lifted Cory's shirt so the bishop could apply holy oil to the affected area. Expecting to see, perhaps, bruised or scratched skin, common with demonic manifestations, what Ralph laid eyes on was unbelievable. Cory's backbone had sunk into his body. It was as if he had no spine and nothing visible holding him up. Seeing this defilement and torture of Cory's body, Bishop McKenna quickly resorted to stronger actions. From the tabernacle behind the altar, he brought out the Holy Eucharist (which Catholics believe is the

Body of Christ) and set it in a monstrance before Cory, who stared at it in a trance-like state. Then the bishop touched Cory's deformed back with holy oil and a variety of relics, each action eliciting a violent jerk.

As the exorcism neared its end, and as Cory's vertebrae reappeared, a silence descended on the chapel for the first time in hours. After a few minutes, Ralph gently asked the clearly-spent musician if he was all right, to which Cory whispered back, "Yes." But then he added something that disheartened everyone. "My spine feels threatened," he said.

Cory was still possessed.

Ralph took him aside and, once again, desperately tried to explain to the withered-looking young man that it was an outside entity causing his problems, not an imbalanced energy field, a blocked chakra, or any other metaphysical "misalignment." A demon—a separate, intelligent, and evil spirit—had taken up residence in his body, and until Cory fully accepted that reality, it couldn't be expelled. But as much as Ralph tried to get this concept across, Cory couldn't grasp it. He would nod affirmatively to everything Ralph said but then contrarily say, "I just don't know what's wrong with me."

Nonetheless, Cory agreed to another exorcism in the near future, and he promised to pray for discernment and deliverance as best he could before then. But in a surprising twist, another exorcism was never needed. Cory called Ralph a few days later and told him he had felt a strong impulse to go to church and sit in the presence of God. He had finally come to realize, he said, that there was an evil—and separate—power present in him, and that he needed to pray for God to banish it from his body. So for two hours, he sat in front of the tabernacle containing the Holy Eucharist and commanded the demon to leave in the name of Jesus Christ, just as Bishop McKenna had done. Incredibly, he felt a surge of energy leave through his spine, the veil lift from his eyes, and a peace fall upon him unlike any he'd ever known, even at the highest levels of TM.

Ralph was convinced that the exorcism performed by Bishop McKenna did work, but the desired effect—the expulsion of the demon—was delayed until Cory truly understood the true nature of his adversary and utilized his free will to confront it. God then stepped in to do the rest.

"There is no time frame in the spirit world or for getting an answer to prayers."

**– Ralph Sarchie, paranormal
investigator/demonologist**

CHAPTER 8

Dangerous Games

In an interview discussing his work as an exorcist for the Archdiocese of Indianapolis, Father Vincent Lampert recounted a story about a mother and father seeking help for their young daughter, who claimed to be having frightening visions of demons. During his visit to their home, Father Lampert noticed the presence of numerous violent and occult-themed video games and a computer with a screensaver depicting a demonic creature. As a first step in assisting their daughter, he suggested that the parents change the screensaver and dispose of the games. They responded by stating that the games were expensive and enjoyable, and so "that wasn't going to happen." When Father Lampert informed them that they needed to be part of the solution and that it wasn't solely about him blessing them and their home with holy water, the family requested that he leave. Thankfully, in the following story, which is based on the experience of a different exorcist, all members of the family agreed to be part of the solution.

* * *

Bill Larkin paced back and forth in his living room as he talked on the phone to the family's parish priest, Father Carl Bowman.

"It's been going on for a couple of weeks now, Father. And it's at the point where she won't even go in or out of her room unless Jeannie or I are with her." He glanced at his wife, who was sitting on the couch, wringing her hands nervously.

Father Bowman listened attentively to Bill's explanation of his daughter's sudden fear of a monster in the house. Seven-year-old Leah had never been the type of child who was afraid of the dark or who imagined monsters under her bed. So her sudden insistence that a big, dark, red-eyed monster with horns was stalking the upstairs hallway definitely captured her parents' attention. As did her screams of terror whenever she "saw" the creature.

"I just don't know what to do, Father. It's heartbreaking to see her so frightened. I think she absolutely believes she is seeing something. Whether it's in her head or not is the question. I know I must sound like a lunatic, but do you think you could come out and, I don't know, say some prayers or something? If nothing else, it would make Leah—and all of us—feel better."

Father Bowman was well-liked in the parish community of St. Anne's. He was known for his quick wit and ability to put people at ease, even those who were suspicious of clergy, and priests in particular. Luckily for the Larkin family, he also had a fair amount of experience in dealing with supernatural situations, which, as he hung up the phone, he couldn't help but think might indeed be the issue in the Larkin house.

Later that afternoon, Father Bowman arrived at the Larkin home. Bill greeted him at the door, with Leah peeking out shyly from behind him. After some small talk and reassurances, Father Bowman asked to be taken to Leah's bedroom. As they walked up the stairs, Bill explained that the monster that Leah saw was always in the hallway. Leah clung to her father's hand tightly as they approached her room.

"What is it doing when you see it, Leah?" the priest asked.

Leah pointed to the end of the hallway, her eyes wide with fear. "It's always down there," she whispered. "And then it comes after me when it sees me."

Father Bowman noticed another door at the end of the hallway where Leah was pointing. He looked at Bill and asked, "What's that room down there?"

"That's my brother's room," Leah answered, emboldened now.

Bill quickly spoke up and reassured the clergyman that his 14-year-old son, Ryan, had nothing to do with this. He was a good kid, a straight-A student who was active in the Boy Scouts and who never caused any trouble. Plus, he loved his little sister and had always been a doting big brother. "He's the perfect teenager, Father. Really."

Father Bowman nodded, but he couldn't shake off a nagging feeling. He had never, in all his years of ministry, encountered a "perfect teenager." He asked if they could see Ryan's room, to which Bill reluctantly agreed.

As they entered Ryan's room, Father Bowman's eyes were immediately drawn to several posters of satanic-themed rock bands on the walls. Bill looked sheepishly at the priest and shrugged. "Kids and their music," he offered weakly. The priest continued looking around the room, noting that it was tidier than he expected a teenage boy's bedroom to be. Then his attention was drawn to the computer desk. Arranged neatly on a shelf above the monitor were numerous cases for video games. Father Bowman pulled one out, stared at it wordlessly for a few moments, and then showed it to Bill. Leah, who was still clutching her father's arm, saw the cover and let out a blood-curdling scream before running out of the room.

Jeannie hurried after her daughter, while Bill and Father Bowman examined the video game case. The game was *Diablo*, a hugely popular video game released in 1997 that had a player battle to rid the world of Diablo, the Lord of Terror. While on this quest, the player journeyed through various netherworld levels before finally entering Hell itself for the ultimate showdown with the demon Diablo. The case cover art that made Leah scream depicted a terrifying horned demon with piercing red eyes surrounded by swirling tendrils of darkness.

"Is it possible Leah has been in Ryan's room while he played this game?" asked Father Bowman.

"I...I don't think so," said Bill. "I'm sure Ryan wouldn't want her to see things like that."

The priest arched an eyebrow. "I don't think anyone should be seeing things like this. Bill, do you know that 'diablo' is Spanish for devil? These games..." He shook his head. "They're not just innocent fun. When you invoke the name of the Evil One, even if you're just doing it in a virtual world, he comes. I think there's a good chance that Ryan inadvertently invited a dark force into your home, and it's manifested as the entity that's been scaring Leah."

Bill was shocked as well as embarrassed. He had always viewed video games as harmless entertainment for his son, but now his lack of vigilance had seemingly made their house a portal to hell. Father Bowman saw the distress on Bill's face and said, "Don't worry. We can take care of this."

Just then, the downstairs door slammed shut, announcing Ryan's arrival home from school. He was surprised to see his dad and Father Bowman in his room, and even more surprised at what they told him they thought was behind Leah's monster sightings.

"But it's just a game," Ryan argued. "People play these games all the time without conjuring up demons."

"They could be without knowing it, Ryan," Father Bowman answered back. "It's fortunate, actually, that in this case the evil showed itself. It usually likes to remain hidden, preying on the weaknesses of its victims, influencing them in bad ways, running down their physical and mental health, and causing all sorts of other problems in their lives. Now we know exactly what we're dealing with."

Ryan remained silent, his gaze fixed on the ground as he appeared to be lost in thought. Then, in a small voice, he admitted that lately when he played the game he felt strange, almost as if he wasn't in control of himself anymore. It was like an outsider was trying to take over. He glanced up at Bill. "There's something else. The other night when I was playing the game, the screen started flickering and I started feeling that weird sensation again. I knew I should stop, but I just couldn't. It was like something was pulling me in deeper." Ryan paused to settle his now-trembling voice. "Then I heard this low growling sound. I thought it was just part of the game, you know? But then the room got super cold, and like a minute later Leah screamed in the hall. I know I should have said something, but I didn't want to make Leah or you guys more upset."

Bill looked at his son with concern, and Father Bowman placed a comforting hand on Ryan's shoulder. "Well, the good news is," the priest said, "it can't have any power over you unless you let it. So, let's get to work and send this thing back to where it belongs."

The first thing Father Bowman instructed Ryan to do was burn the *Diablo* game, along with a couple of similar games, and also the satanic rock posters. Bill helped him complete that task in the garage, while Jeannie and Leah watched from a safe distance. Afterward, Father Bowman performed a rite of minor exorcism on Ryan's room and computer. Then he went through the house, sprinkling holy water and reciting deliverance prayers in all the rooms and hallways. Finally, he had Ryan formally renounce his association with the game and with any demonic entity that had attached itself to the family through it.

As he was packing up to leave, Father Bowman offered a final bit of advice to the Larkins: "This is just the beginning now. You have to keep up these resolutions. Invite the good in to keep the evil out." He cast a knowing look at Bill. "Regular Sunday Mass attendance is a good start." Then he turned to Ryan and said with a wink, "I hear Super Mario is fun." Ryan rolled his eyes and laughed.

That night, as her parents tucked her into bed, Leah asked, "Is the monster really gone?"

Her mother smoothed back her hair and said gently, "Yes, sweetheart, Father Bowman made sure of it. No more monsters in the hallway."

Reassured, Leah snuggled under her covers. Within minutes, she was sound asleep, the peaceful rhythm of her breathing untroubled by any visions or nightmares.

Down the hall, Ryan too found restful sleep instead of the lurid dreams that had haunted him of late. A tranquil energy settled over the house, the dark of the night no longer menacing, just a momentary break before the bright light of the day came to rule.

"There is a growing trend, I think, to see the exorcist as a magician, that somehow I have a bag of tricks that can make people's problems go away. But again, it's not about just casting the devil out. It's also about inviting God in. I would even say that casting the devil out is the easy part."

– Fr. Vincent Lampert, exorcist for the Archdiocese of Indianapolis

CHAPTER 9

Tarot Card Terror

Tarot cards originated in the mid-14th century in Europe, primarily as a set of cards used for a game known as Trionfi. The cards evolved over the centuries, incorporating allegorical and symbolic imagery, and in the late 18th century began to be used for divination and occult purposes. The deck as we know it today consists of 22 cards known as the Major Arcana, whose figures represent a synthesis of the mysteries of life, and 56 cards known as the Minor Arcana, whose images incorporate 14 figures in four series (gold, clubs, swords, and goblets).

Like all other forms of divination, once the practice starts and becomes habitual, the spirits that come through eventually gain greater control over their victims. In some cases that control is manifested right away, and in other cases, like in the following story, it is hidden until many, many years later.

* * *

The old weathered cards slid out of the worn leather case, their edges frayed and the designs faded from years of use. Cara's grandmother carefully laid them out on the small wooden table, her gnarled fingers delicately tracing the intricate patterns.

Cara watched in rapt attention as Nana flipped the cards over one by one, her brow furrowed in concentration. The young girl perched on the edge of the worn armchair, not daring to make a sound lest she disturb the ritual.

Nana's voice was low and soothing as she began to interpret the spread, her words lilting with the cadence of a well-rehearsed performance. Cara listened, enraptured, as her grandmother described the various symbols and their meanings, her mind conjuring vivid images to match the cryptic messages.

The sound of the doorbell jolted them both, breaking the spell. Nana gave Cara's hand a gentle squeeze before rising stiffly and making her way to the front door. Cara remained seated, fixing her gaze on the cards and tracing the worn edges with her fingers as if she could divine their secrets.

Soon, the low murmur of voices drifted in from the other room, and Cara knew Nana's client had arrived. She moved to a darkened corner where she would remain silent and still so as to not be a distraction for either Nana or the client. From there, she would listen to the familiar ritual unfold—the shuffling of the cards, the murmured questions, the thoughtful pauses.

Cara longed to be a part of it, to immerse herself in the mystical world of her grandmother's craft and do readings for people. She was too young right now, Nana kept telling her. "Someday, child. Someday." Cara loved her grandmother and trusted her words. For now, she would simply be content to keep learning at Nana's knee, and someday, if the fates allowed, she herself would be privy to the mysteries of the Tarot.

As fate would have it, though, Cara was not to become a tarot master any time soon. Nana passed away quietly in her sleep when Cara was ten, and as the years passed, Cara's fascination with her grandmother's mysterious craft began to wane. The once captivating world of tarot cards and cryptic readings faded into the background, replaced by the more mundane concerns of adolescence. School, soccer, slumber parties, and the occasional crush on a boy filled her days and nights, leaving little room for the esoteric pursuits of her early childhood.

As Cara entered her teenage years, she discovered a passion for theater, throwing herself into school plays and community theater productions. Her natural talent for embodying a wide variety of characters, as well as her dedication to the less glamorous aspects of the field, earned her praise from directors and fellow actors alike. It was not surprising, then, that when it came time for college, Cara chose theater arts as her major.

As she packed her bags and prepared to leave home for the first time, Cara stumbled upon the old leather case containing her grandmother's tarot cards. She paused for a moment, running her fingers over the worn surface before tucking it back into the closet. That part of her life was a distant memory, yet when she touched the case, an odd sensation came over her that she couldn't explain. Visceral memories of Nana, she supposed. A thought continued to nag her, though, even during the drive to her new campus residence. Why would Nana's memory send a cold shiver through her body?

Cara's first year of college flew by in a whirlwind of classes, rehearsals, and performances. Her professors praised her talent and dedication, and she quickly became a standout among her peers. When she wasn't studying or performing, Cara spent time with her boyfriend, Derek, an accounting major who shared her love for the theater but who also kept her grounded in the real world.

As her second year began, Cara found herself settling into a comfortable routine. In addition to Derek, she had a close-knit group of friends, mostly fellow theater majors, with whom she spent time both on and off campus. One crisp autumn evening, Cara and a few of her friends gathered in the living room of their shared apartment for a "girls' night" of relaxation and fun. Laughter and chatter filled the air as the friends caught up on the latest gossip and swapped stories from their classes and rehearsals. After a while, one of the girls, a bubbly redhead named Jenna, pulled out a small velvet pouch from her bag.

"Check out what I found at the thrift store today," Jenna announced. She carefully emptied the contents of the pouch onto the coffee table, revealing a pristine set of tarot cards and an illustrated instruction manual. "They're like brand new! I couldn't pass them up."

The girls leaned in, intrigued by the intricately designed cards and eager to try them out. It wasn't long before they were using their theatrical voices to act out comedic vignettes of mysterious gypsy fortune tellers and their spellbound clients.

Cara, who had been in the kitchen grabbing snacks, walked into the living room and stopped short at the sight of the cards spread out on the table. A flood of memories washed over her as she recalled the countless hours she had spent watching her grandmother perform readings.

"Oh, I know what that is!" Cara exclaimed, a smile spreading across her face as she pointed to an upturned card on the table. "My grandmother read these cards all the time. I can tell you exactly what they mean."

She sat down facing the cards.

"This one," she said, tapping a card depicting a hooded figure, "is the Hermit. It represents solitude, introspection, and seeking deeper wisdom." Her gaze shifted to the next card. "And this one is the Wheel of Fortune—change, cycles, and the ebb and flow of life."

The girls watched, enthralled, as Cara continued to interpret each card in a low and soothing voice, her words lilting with the cadence of a well-rehearsed performance. For a few seconds, Cara was taken outside of herself, listening to the rhythmic and mesmerizing voice of her grandmother at a table reading in a darkened little back room from ages ago. It was as if Nana's spirit had taken hold of her, guiding her words and lending them an almost mystical quality.

When she had finished, the room fell silent, the girls staring at her with a mixture of awe and wonder. Cara blinked, suddenly self-conscious, and a faint blush crept across her cheeks.

"I... I don't know where that came from," she admitted, her fingers tracing the edge of the tarot deck.

Cara had no sooner said these words when her body suddenly stiffened, her eyes rolled back in her head, and the lights in the room started flickering. A thunderous boom echoed in the room. Then an unearthly voice came from Cara and said, "Stupid witch! Stupid witch! I had to wait in her for 20 years for her to make the first move."

The deep, guttural voice that issued forth from Cara's lips sent chills down the spines of the gathered friends. Jenna and the others scrambled backward, knocking over the coffee table and sending the tarot cards flying in all directions.

"What's happening?" Jenna cried, her voice shaking with terror.

Cara's body then began contorting unnaturally, her limbs thrashing about as if being pulled by invisible strings. The flickering lights cast an eerie glow upon the scene, casting dancing shadows like some hellish parody of a classical ballet.

"We have to help her!" one of the other girls shouted, but no one dared to approach the convulsing young woman.

The unearthly voice echoed through the room once more, dripping with malice. "You can't help her. She's mine now. Just like her Nana."

Suddenly, Cara's body went rigid, and a sinister laugh bubbled up from deep within her. The girls watched in horror as her features began to shift and contort, her face taking on a demonic, inhuman quality. They huddled together, clutching one another in sheer terror. One of the girls, Lily, said in a hushed voice, "I think we should pray." The others nodded in agreement, not sure what else to do. They grasped each other's hands and slowly began reciting the Our Father. Their voices were tenuous at first but grew louder and firmer with each repetition of the prayer. Eventually, the fiendish noises coming from Cara quieted, the lights stopped flickering, and a calm descended on the room. The girls looked up from their bowed positions just in time to see Cara collapse on the floor.

"What happened?" Cara asked bewilderedly after her friends rushed to her aid. The girls looked at each other. Who was going to tell her?

The campus chaplain, Reverend Hayes, listened intently as Cara recounted the previous night's horrific events, as much as she could, at least, from what her friends had told her. She still didn't remember any of it herself. Derek had come with her and was now holding her slightly trembling hand.

When she had finished, Reverend Hayes gave her an encouraging smile.

"Well, Cara, I've got good news and bad news. How about the bad news first?"

Cara nodded.

"Okay. It sounds like you've got an unwanted guest. An evil spirit, a demon, has likely attached itself to you through those cards. Like a Ouija board, the Tarot acts as an invitation to these dark spirits. They hear the call and will gladly act at your behest…at first. Your grandmother, for example, may have believed a good spirit guide or even her intuitive subconscious was leading her to read the cards. But we know from experience—many experiences similar to yours—that this is usually not the case."

Cara felt her stomach twist into knots. She had so many fond memories of her grandmother's readings, never realizing the danger she had been exposed to as a child.

"The demon," Reverend Hayes continued, "has been with you all this time, waiting for the right moment to manifest. And when you began interpreting the cards last night, you unwittingly gave it the permission it needed to take control."

Derek squeezed Cara's hand reassuringly. "But how do we get rid of it?" he asked.

"Well, that's the good news. We have a deliverance session scheduled for tomorrow night in the chapel. You'd be surprised how many young people have difficulties similar to yours."

"So, you're talking about an exorcism?" Cara felt a shiver run down her spine. The thought of having a demon inside her was terrifying enough, but the idea of an exorcism filled her with dread. She couldn't imagine what that would entail.

Reverend Hayes sensed her unease. "I know this is a lot to take in, Cara. But I promise you, with faith and the power of God's love, we can cast this thing out. Good always wins over evil."

Cara nodded, her eyes brimming with tears. Derek pulled her close, offering silent support. She cried as much for her Nana as she did for herself. Had she been deceived all those years, or did she know? She tried to shake those thoughts out of her head. Right now she had to deal with her own demon. She hugged Derek tightly and resolved to fight the nefarious intruder before it upended her life.

Cara returned to her apartment that evening feeling a mix of apprehension and determination. Reverend Hayes had prayed over her before she left his office, but he warned her that the demon may be "active" leading up to the deliverance service, knowing that its time was nearly up. She needed to be on guard and maintain a positive attitude.

Sure enough, as if a script were playing out, the first thing Cara noticed when she entered her home was a lone tarot card lying on the floor. It was the Death card. Despite the ominous sight, Cara couldn't help but chortle and say out loud, "Really? A little dramatic, don't you think?" Her insides, however, were fluttering. Where did the card come from? Did she accidentally bring one of Jenna's home after the party and drop it? Without further hesitation, she picked up the card and carried it to the kitchen sink, found a match, and burned it. Then she turned every light on in the house, grabbed the Bible Reverend Hayes had given her, and spent the evening reading and praying. When the lights began flickering around midnight, just as she was trying to go to sleep, she called Derek and asked him to keep her company. Thankfully, the only disturbance she experienced after Derek arrived was the sound of his snoring from the couch.

Cara attended the deliverance service the following night, as well as several follow-up sessions with Reverend Hayes. The demon never manifested again, nor was Cara bothered by obsessive thoughts, physical attacks, or any other paranormal events that could suggest the presence of an evil entity. She graduated with a degree in theater arts and married Derek a year later. She remains thankful that her experience was not only short-lived but also eye-opening to the dangers of the occult. As she learned, victims aren't always the practitioners. Sometimes they're the bystanders.

"After getting rid of them, I realized the cards had actually connected me with 'something,' as I started to feel a presence which kept coming to me, very often, almost weekly. It came at any time … because I had finally broken the connection, and it was trying to keep it."

– Tina, former tarot card user

CHAPTER 10

The Haunted Farm

While oftentimes people turn to witchcraft and magic for fame, fortune, love, or some other self-centered motive, some are driven to these esoteric practices out of desperation. A loved one is sick. Financial ruin looms. Or a curse is feared and protective retaliation is deemed necessary. The unfortunate result, however, of falling for magic's deceitful allure is that the promised solution, even if granted for a period of time, invariably summons even greater calamity into the lives of the supplicants.

* * *

In 1933, Reverend Franz Walther embarked from his native Germany on a mission to France. It wasn't long before his reputation for preaching, healing, and "chasser le diable," or "driving out the devil," brought throngs of attendees to his services. Following one such spirited gathering, a man hesitantly approached Franz, accompanied by his visibly troubled wife and their teenage son. With a trembling voice, the man introduced himself as Marcel and proceeded to tell Franz a troubling account of horrors that had befallen his family.

They hailed from a modest farm nestled in the heart of the Vosges Mountains. For as long as Marcel could remember, going back even to his boyhood days, the farm had been plagued by a series of inexplicable and unsettling super-natural occurrences. Shadows that moved without any apparent source, whispers that echoed in empty rooms, and objects that would inexplicably shift or fall grew to be a grim part of their everyday lives.

In addition to these bizarre phenomena, several of their cows had periodically experienced symptoms of a mysterious paralysis, a nightmarish affliction that had also besieged Marcel intermittently. Despite numerous attempts to find natural explanations for these events, no answers could ever be found. Nor could it be understood why the cows frequently exhibited intense fear and restlessness in their stables, often bellowing into the night as if sensing an unseen predator.

Marcel's father, driven to desperation by these unrelenting issues, had been compelled to sell all but one of the cows, a heart-wrenching decision that left him teetering on the brink of financial ruin. It was at this point, with his livelihood hanging by a thread, that his father decided to go outside the normal channels of aid—after all, nothing he had tried so far had helped—and sought the assistance of a man who practiced sorcery. The man, who went by the name Lucien, came out to the farm and performed a series of bizarre rituals around the stables—chanting incantations, drawing mystical symbols in the dirt, and burning strange herbs. In the months that followed, the family's livestock troubles ceased, and a seemingly more peaceful air descended upon the household.

Unfortunately, the outbreak of World War I brought a new upheaval to Marcel's family. They were forced to abandon their farm for several years while the French military requisitioned the land in their region for tactical purposes.

When the conflict finally ended, the family returned with renewed hope for the future, along with three new members: Marcel's wife and two young children.

However, their respite was short-lived as the mysterious disturbances from Marcel's childhood started up again, this time with a more sinister edge. A malevolent force, unseen but palpable, launched a brutal attack on the family, pushing them down stairs, scratching their skin, and branding them with inexplicable burns. Even the children were not safe from the onslaught, enduring constant injuries and illnesses that no doctor could alleviate or cure.

Desperate to protect his family from harm or even death, Marcel decided to take the same action his father took years ago to save the family cows: hire a sorcerer. Though the magician that his father used no longer resided in the area, another spellcaster was recommended to Marcel by local townspeople. This man, a shopkeeper by day who practiced magic at night, was more than happy to assist—for the right price and the understanding that his "work" was not guaranteed. Marcel nonetheless agreed, and the next day the sorcerer arrived at the farm with his ceremonial garments, various herbs and potions, and a tattered ritual book. His incantations seemed to work at first. The oldest child regained his vitality overnight, and to his parents' delight, he played the next day with no distress or disturbances. But tragically, their second child only got worse, his breathing becoming more labored and agonizing until he finally succumbed to his mystery malady at the age of six weeks.

Marcel himself was plagued in much the same way, and despite undergoing extensive medical tests and treatments, he could never get a clear diagnosis as to what was making him sick so often. There was another matter vexing Marcel as well, but this one he dared not tell any doctor for fear they would find him mad. At night, he was relentlessly tormented by the horrifying sensation of being lifted into the air by invisible hands and forcefully thrown back down onto his bed, leaving him bruised and battered by morning. Other unsettling occurrences were happening throughout the house. A strong, nauseating odor permeated the entire household; peculiar noises echoed day and night, including the eerie sound of doors opening and closing by themselves; and frigid areas of cold would inexplicably materialize in any given room despite the scorching summer temperatures.

Several years went by with Marcel and his family enduring these tribulations until finally one night, Marcel, having grown thin and emaciated from his ordeals, tried to seek solace in prayer, something he had not practiced since he was a young boy. Clutching an old prayer book, he sat down at a nearby table and desperately called upon God to deliver him from his torment. Suddenly, an immense force gripped the lower part of his body, lifted him up, and slammed him back down onto his chair with such violence that he feared he might burst from the impact.

Terrified that this unseen, powerful force would soon kill him or a loved one, and receiving no immediate relief from his brief attempt at prayer, Marcel once again called upon a witchcraft practitioner to assist him. As before, soon after the sorcerer had performed his rituals, the conditions in Marcel's household did improve. Marcel regained his health, and the unexplained strange phenomena subsided. But also like previous times, the sorcerer's magic only lasted so long before its promised effect wore off, and bigger trouble ensued. The family's livestock was once again smitten with debilitating physical conditions. Their fields turned barren, and what food they had stored became beset with bugs and rot.

Most distressingly, Marcel's son began experiencing the same malicious assaults on his body as he did years ago as a young child. At first, it was no more than waking up with a few scratches or welts on his arms and legs. But then it turned to pushing, pinching, and slapping during the day by some invisible entity. Finally, right after he turned fifteen, the boy began to experience even more terrifying things, claiming to see monstrous figures lurking in the shadows and stalking the halls of their home. One morning, as the teen was rising from his bed, he was suddenly seized by an unseen force, its grip so powerful that it left his right arm completely paralyzed. Marcel sought medical treatment for his son's paralysis, but as always, no doctor could offer an explanation or solution. When he heard about Reverend Franz Walther's healing mission, although he still had doubts about the efficacy of prayer, Marcel knew he had to try it, as all other options had failed miserably.

As Marcel was telling the clergyman his harrowing story, Franz noticed that the son's arm hung limply at his side and appeared devoid of any muscle tone or functionality. It also became abundantly clear to Franz what lay behind the dreadful events that had befallen the family. After Marcel finished his account, Franz told them of the terrible consequences that can arise from engaging with the dark arts of magic and sorcery. In a dire case such as theirs, he explained, no doctor could provide the help they needed, but only Christ Himself, who alone was the true victor over the powers of darkness. Then he urged them to repent of their past misdeeds and to turn to God with their whole heart and soul.

Marcel, his wife, and his son immediately agreed, pledging their lives to God in that very moment before the minister and a small crowd of congregants. Then Franz prayed over the boy with a fervency that seemed to draw down the very essence of divine power. As witnesses recounted, the boy's arm was suddenly healed, regaining its strength and mobility before their very eyes. A few days later, he was even helping his father in the fields with his newly restored strength.

From that time forth, Marcel, his family, and his farm experienced no further malevolent disturbances or unexplained ill health. The air of the farm, once heavy with despair, was now light with renewed hope and tranquility. Interestingly, years later during the Second World War, Franz's family was forced to evacuate from Strasbourg and found shelter with Marcel's family. Despite the raging turmoil of war all around them, an otherworldly peace remained at hand within the walls of that once-tempestuous mountain home.

"The help of magic is only an apparent help. It merely shifts the load to another area. A small relief in one department is paid for by an excessive stress in another. The compensation is far in excess of the help one apparently experiences. Satan cheats his victims every time."

– Dr. Kurt E. Koch, theologian and author

Chapter 11

The Witching Well

Exorcism is usually thought of as the remedy for a possessed person. But it can also be necessary when an object or place is infested with demonic spirits. Dwellings become infested for a number of reasons, including the use of the location for occult activities such as séances or witchcraft, or for criminal activities such as drug dealing or prostitution. It could be that a murder or suicide took place on the property. Or the home may contain a cursed item or have been cursed itself. Whatever the cause, the effect can range from troubling to terrifying. Father Gabriele Amorth, formerly the chief exorcist of Rome, recalled that his worst cases stemmed from satanic rituals. The resultant disturbances were so great, and the task of expelling the demons so difficult, that he was sometimes forced to recommend that people simply pack their bags and leave.

* * *

1893

Beneath the luminous glow of the full moon, a circle of hooded figures cloaked in dark robes encircled the ancient and abandoned well, their faces obscured by the shadows that danced amongst the flickering flames of the black candles they held in their trembling hands. The air was thick with an aura of wicked anticipation, the eerie quiet broken only by an occasional chilling breeze or the mournful hoot of an owl.

At the stroke of midnight, the deep silence was broken by the haunting melody of a single flute. The cloaked figures began to sway to the somber tune, their fluttering candles casting crazy shadows upon the well's crumbling façade. From their midst stepped forward the coven's high priest, his face hidden behind a demonic mask of feathers and horns. Lifting his chin to the heavens, he began chanting in an ancient tongue. The others joined in the incantation, their voices strong and unwavering in their united supplication.

From behind a grove of trees, another hooded figure led a braying goat to the center of the group. As the dark disciple untied the animal's leash, four others placed a heavy stone slab across the top of the well. Together, they lifted the terrified animal onto the makeshift altar and tied its feet together, forcing it to lie helplessly on its side as it awaited its fate.

The high priest drew from his robe a large jewel-encrusted dagger and approached the altar. He raised his hands high to quiet the crowd and garner their attention.

"Tonight we offer this sacrifice to our dark lord to gain his favor and blessings. We shall do his bidding and he shall reward us! Hail Satan!"

"Hail Satan!" the crowd repeated.

"Come close, fellow servants of Satan. Come and be sanctified with the blood of the offering."

The coven members set down their candles, shed their robes, and drew near to the altar, naked and trembling with excitement. The high priest murmured under his breath and then drove the dagger into the goat with a fury as from hell itself. Over and over he stabbed at the bucking animal, its blood spraying in every direction onto the enraptured crowd. At last the goat stopped moving, and the high priest, his chest heaving from exertion, muttered the words, "It is done."

The flames of the candles surged higher, casting capricious shapes upon the now-writhing bodies of the coven members who fell atop each other in a bacchanalian frenzy. Meanwhile, the blood of the sacrifice seeped through the cracks in the altar stone and dripped down into the darkened depths of the old well, soon to be forgotten as time dispersed the people of the full moon and as new edifices were built over old.

2010

The scream pierced her dream-laden skull like a spike being driven into a railroad tie. Kathy jolted awake, her heart pounding. Beside her, Rick stirred, mumbling incoherently. She shook him urgently.

"Rick! Wake up. I think that was Ethan."

Kathy leapt from the bed, her bare feet slapping against the hardwood floors. She raced down the hall to Ethan's room and flung open the door. Her five-year-old son was sitting upright in bed, cheeks wet with tears, blankets tangled around his legs.

"Ethan! What's wrong?" Kathy rushed over and enveloped him in her arms.

"The monster," Ethan whimpered. "He was standing in the corner again."

Kathy's gaze darted around the moonlit room. Nothing but shadows. She reached over and turned on the bedside lamp. Furniture and toys instantly materialized, their familiarity reassuring.

"No monsters, honey. It was probably just a shadow. Our minds play tricks on us when we're half asleep."

She cradled Ethan in her arms, gently running her fingers through his hair as his little frame shook with fear.

Rick appeared in the doorway. "Another nightmare?"

Kathy nodded. This was the third night in a row. As she met Rick's gaze, she knew they shared the same thoughts. It wasn't just the nightmares that were a concern. The past few weeks had been plagued by strange occurrences—lights flickering, odd noises, shadows darting just out of sight. It was hard to deny anymore that they were all connected. The question now was, why? Why, after eight months of undisturbed, peaceful living in their dream farmhouse were they having these distressing disturbances in their lives?

Over the next few days, the unsettling incidents in the house escalated. Kathy walked into the kitchen one morning to find that all of her cookbooks had been knocked off their shelf and lay scattered on the floor. Rick's keys went missing another day, making him late for work as he spent the better part of an hour looking for them before they "showed up" in the pantry. While these incidents had the couple scratching their heads, it wasn't until Ethan's favorite teddy bear ended up in the trash bin, its arm torn off and the stuffing ripped out of its belly, that Rick and Kathy considered the possibility that they were dealing with something supernatural—and malicious.

Possibility turned to certainty a couple of nights later when Ethan's bloodcurdling scream ripped through the house once again. Kathy and Rick bolted from their bed and raced to their son's room. They found him thrashing on the bed, trapped in an unrelenting visceral nightmare.

"Wake up, Ethan," Kathy said, shaking him gently. "It's just a dream."

Ethan's eyes flew open, wide and haunted. He clung to his mother, his small body shaking violently.

As Kathy held him close, she noticed something dark on his pajama shirt. She gently turned him around and gasped in horror. Three clearly distinct red scratches marred the soft skin of his back. Not just scratches, Kathy thought to herself. Claw marks.

"Rick, look at this," she whispered, her voice trembling.

Rick leaned in, his face paling as he saw the marks. "What the hell?"

Ethan whimpered, burying his face in Kathy's chest. "The monster did it. He said he's going to take me away."

Kathy and Rick exchanged a look of pure fear. This was no longer just a case of juvenile night terrors or strange coincidences. Nor was it a poltergeist, an idea they had recently considered. No, something more sinister than a mischievous ghost was at work. And it had its sights set on their son.

The next morning, Kathy sat at the kitchen table with her laptop open as she scoured paranormal forums and websites. Rick came up behind her, placing a hand on her shoulder.

"Any luck?"

Kathy shook her head. "According to these so-called experts, we could have ghosts, demons, imps, aliens, or mice."

"Mice didn't do that to Ethan."

Kathy sighed and closed the laptop. "I know. Just trying to lighten the mood."

"You know, what we should probably do is—"

Just then, Ethan came bounding into the room, full of his usual five-year-old energy.

"Hey kiddo, ready for school?" Rick asked, scooping Ethan up and eliciting a burst of giggles. Watching them, Kathy felt a swell of love and protectiveness, as well as gratitude that Ethan, in typical child-like fashion, had moved on from last night's fright.

After dropping Ethan off at kindergarten, Kathy drove her usual route back home, but this time her eyes were drawn to the Catholic church, St. Patrick's, that she passed every day but really never thought about. She and Rick were not religious, nor were they brought up in any specific religious tradition. Nonetheless, she felt a pull toward the spiral-topped structure that she couldn't explain. Why not? she thought. In the movies, priests were always the ones called in to deal with evil spirits and haunted houses. If that didn't characterize her family's situation right now, she didn't know what did.

Kathy walked into the parish office, the bright white, modern design taking her a little by surprise. She was expecting something more old-fashioned, more "churchy," and immediately started second-guessing her reason for being there. Would they think she was crazy? Thankfully, the parish secretary quickly put her at ease, assuring her that "priests do house blessings all the time." Though there weren't any priests available at that time, the woman took down Kathy's information and said she'd have one of them arrange a visit. Kathy silently hoped that a blessing was all they needed, but truth be told, she had her doubts.

Father Adams arrived at the house the next night, just after dinner. Rick showed him into the living room where Kathy sat on the couch, hugging her knees to her chest. Ethan played on the floor, pushing a toy truck around and making little engine noises. After introductions were made, Father Adams took a seat in the armchair. He had a kind face, etched with lines that spoke of experience beyond his years.

"So, tell me about these strange occurrences," he prompted gently.

Kathy and Rick took turns relaying the events of the past few weeks: the nightmares, the flickering lights, the misplaced objects. When they got to the part about the claw marks on Ethan's back, Father Adams leaned forward, his brow furrowed with concern.

"May I see them?" he asked.

Kathy nodded and called Ethan over. The boy climbed into his mother's lap as she lifted his shirt. The angry red lines stood out in stark contrast to his pale skin.

Father Adams sat back, stroking his chin thoughtfully. "I did some research on this house before I came out here tonight."

Rick and Kathy exchanged a glance. They knew the house had had an unusually high number of short-term residents, but their realtor had just shrugged it off as a sign of the times. People move around a lot, he had said.

Father Adams continued. "So I'm sure you know the house was built in 1946. It was a post-war project for a returning serviceman. He had hoped to raise his family here and maybe turn it into a little hobby farm. But unfortunately, five years later, he committed suicide in the grove of trees out back. The newspaper attributed it to 'shell shock.'"

Kathy's hand flew to her mouth. "That's awful."

Father Adams nodded. "After his wife and children moved back west to live with her parents, the house went through a series of owners, none of them staying longer than a few years. There's an old fella in my parish who remembers the locals talking about how the land was cursed."

"Because of the suicide?" Kathy asked.

"No. Before that. It seems there's been—" The priest paused, casting a glance at Ethan before lowering his voice to continue. "—rumors of witches in these parts."

"Witches?!" Kathy was incredulous. "That's crazy. Everyone we've met here has been wonderful to us. You can't be serious, Father?"

"Well, we're talking about a long time ago. I doubt there are any practitioners around here now. Of course, you never know. It's not like they walk around in pointy hats and black robes." He smiled at the jest, but seeing only dismay on his listeners' faces, he quickly changed the subject.

"Why don't I look around, if that's all right? Get a feel for the energy here."

While Kathy entertained Ethan, Rick walked through the house with Father Adams. At one point, the priest asked Rick if he ever felt like he was being watched.

"Actually, yes. I didn't bring it up because I figured with everything else going on, it was just my mind playing tricks on me."

Father Adams nodded. "What you've been feeling is real. I felt it as soon as I came into the house, and it's only been getting stronger. Whatever it is, it definitely doesn't like me being here."

The last stop in the house was the basement. As the two men descended the stairs, a cold rush of air brushed their faces.

"That's weird. There aren't any open windows down here," Rick said.

When they reached the bottom, their senses were attacked again, this time with a strong, foul stench of rotting meat.

"Yew!" said Rick, pinching his nose. "I've never noticed that before. I wonder if something died down here."

"It's reacting to me," Father Adams said calmly.

"It?" Rick asked.

Choosing not to answer, the priest asked, "So have you ever found anything down here that seemed unusual? Something old, perhaps, or out of place?"

"Everything's old in this house." Rick thought for a minute. "But there is something a little different. An old town well was right below here. The realtor assured us it was filled in and sealed properly, and since it's back there under the steps, it's never been something we've really thought about." He led the priest to a shadowy spot beneath the staircase and pointed his flashlight at a large cylindrical stone structure that protruded about a foot out of the ground. "Supposedly it dates back to Civil War times," Rick said, brushing dirt off the weathered top with his hand. "Looking at these hieroglyphics, or whatever they are, I'd say it dates farther back than that."

Father Adams stooped and stared at the symbols that had been etched in the well's stonework.

"Those are occult symbols," said Father Adams. "And I would bet anything that this—" He traced his finger over several patches of dark rust-colored stains. "—is blood."

"Blood? Like, human blood?"

"Possibly," said the priest. "Or animal blood. The sacrifice of animals is rather common among those who practice black magic."

A loud crash and clatter from the other side of the basement made the two men jump in surprise.

"What the—?" Rick stared in disbelief as hundreds of nails bounced and scattered chaotically along the ground. In their midst lay a shattered plastic storage box that had moments before been safely ensconced on a shelf above.

"It's manifesting," Father Adams said solemnly.

"What? What's manifesting?"

"The demon. There's a demon in this house, Rick. From everything you've told me, and what I've seen and felt myself, there's no doubt. The source is most likely this well. I'm guessing those rumors of witches were more than just rumors, and this is where they did their rituals."

"But why now? We've lived here for eight months and haven't had any problems."

"Evil spirits are very patient, Rick. They watch and wait, formulating their plans on how best to terrorize their victims without fully exposing themselves. They've been doing this for eons, remember."

Just then, a nail flew through the air and hit Rick on the arm. A tiny prick mark began to ooze blood.

Father Adams grabbed his other arm and ushered him toward the steps. "We better get out of here. It knows its time is almost up and it will be more active than usual."

Racing up the stairs, Rick muttered to himself. *A demon? You've got to be kidding me.*

On the advice of Father Adams, Rick, Kathy, and Ethan spent the night at a hotel. The next day, while Ethan was in school, Father Adams and another priest, Father Yang, returned and performed an exorcism of the house and, in particular, of the well. When the family returned home a few hours later, they immediately noticed that the air in the house felt less "heavy." Father Adams assured them it wasn't their imagination. He felt it too, a sense of lightness and peace. These were good signs, he said, that the exorcism was successful.

He then apologized to Rick and Kathy for the large black stain on the basement wall. He explained that near the end of the Rite, as the priests were commanding the demon to leave, a black shapeless mass materialized from under the staircase, glided across the room, and disappeared through the wall, leaving the mysterious residue.

The family experienced no further paranormal activity after that, but did end up moving to a different town two years later after Rick was offered a better job. This time, Rick and Kathy narrowed their dream home choices to only newly constructed houses.

"Before you begin a paranormal investigation, the most important criteria you need to gather is the back history of the location."

– Zak Bagans, paranormal investigator and host of
Ghost Adventures

CHAPTER 12

The Tree Troll

In the last account, it was noted that demonic infestations of dwellings occur either because of occult activity or illicit and violent doings on the premises. There is another reason for demonic disturbances, however, that is more often a phenomenon in cultures with strong folk religiosity, and that is the presence of elementals, or nature spirits. These spirits, according to most exorcists, are demons that reside in old trees, mounds, forests, lakes, caves, mountains, and other natural habitats.

They show themselves in different forms (elves, dwarves, goblins, fairies, gnomes, nymphs, Olympian gods, etc.) depending on the culture and mythology of the place they reside, and they almost always appear in the same form so that they may be recognized and given due reverence. Sometimes they manifest because someone has invoked them for protection or luck. At other times, it is because their land has been disturbed during construction and they feel entitled to appropriate the resultant new structure. They are easily offended, and they will punish severely, with sickness or even death, those who brazenly intrude into their territory.

Filipino exorcists are kept quite busy with these *malignos* or *engkantos*, with some clergy even experiencing rather personal connections. Father Jose Francisco C. Syquia, the chief exorcist for the Archdiocese of Manila, first encountered these creatures before he was ordained a priest. His story, as told below, was an eye-opening experience and one that undoubtedly helped groom him for his future assignment as an exorcist.

* * *

Jose's childhood residence was a two-story house constructed in the 1950s. His family moved in during the early 1970s, when life in Makati, now the financial hub of the Philippines, was still tranquil and unhurried. As a young boy, Jose would occasionally overhear the household staff recounting tales of mysterious and eerie occurrences inside and outside the house that they couldn't explain. Jose would usually only catch snippets of these stories from his brother Martin, who was more outgoing and frequently conversed with the staff.

Over the years, Jose frequently heard the same accounts of *duwendes* (mischievous dwarf-like creatures) seen around the house. They were reportedly seen playing on the swing set and even swimming in the pool. At the time, he did not take these stories seriously, particularly as he never saw any of the creepy little goblins himself or otherwise experienced any supernatural phenomena. His perception changed, however, one night when Martin had some friends over for a sleepover.

Of the many stories whispered among staff, one of the most consistent was that of an entity that roamed the house at night, especially on the ground floor where the bedrooms were often unoccupied. One hot summer night, Martin and some friends used one of these bedrooms for their sleepover. However, no one slept very well, if at all. Martin couldn't sleep, he later said, because he sensed that there was a malevolent entity closely observing him. After struggling silently with his fears for more than an hour, he finally realized that all his friends were also wide awake and sensing the same sinister presence. The boys unanimously agreed to move to another part of the house.

This and the numerous other strange incidents talked about over the years gradually convinced Jose that something paranormal was occurring in the house. But it wasn't until many years later, when he was a seminarian, that he and Martin decided to delve a little deeper and, with the help of a deliverance team, purge their ancestral abode of any and all troublesome spirits.

The plan began as scheduled, with the deliverance team arriving early in the evening while there was still plenty of light. Jose hurried to the gate to welcome them. The team consisted of Father Jay, the team leader; Sister Rose, a green-habited nun who specialized in spiritual warfare; and several lay people.

Jose's first clue of what was to come was when Sister Rose exited the van and immediately doubled over in pain and began vomiting. He looked at her with confusion, not yet realizing that she was sensitive to the spirit world and reacting to an evil presence nearby. He became more alarmed when she showed the group her arms—and the rash that was spreading on them like wildfire. She looked truly sick, and Jose feared she might collapse right there on the spot. But a few minutes later, she waved off the ministrations of those who had gathered around her and assured them she was all right. "Let's get to work," she said. Although Jose was still somewhat skeptical about a spiritual explanation for her condition, he gradually came to understand that these physical maladies were indeed a form of spiritual harassment.

The team decided to split up. Jose accompanied Father Jay toward the dimly lit storage area and driveway on the left side of the home. Sister Rose, with the rest of the group, left to investigate the central grounds of the estate. Father Jay wore his stole and carried a bottle of holy water, which he sprinkled vigorously in the different corners of the driveway area. But as Jose led the priest into the darker corners near a large storage shed, Father Jay began to exhibit signs of pain.

Grimacing and shaking his right arm, the priest said, "There are entities here. My arm is reacting negatively." Jose looked at him confusedly, unsure of how to respond. Without further explanation but seemingly nonplussed, Father Jay continued blessing the area with holy water.

Upon entering the large, dark shed, Jose could practically taste the dry and stagnant air. The dark silhouettes of numerous boxes were visible, and Jose couldn't help but wonder what else was in there with them. This particular storage area was rarely visited, maybe once or twice a year when items needed to be stored away for the long haul. Even though he was not psychic or spirit-sensitive, Jose began feeling a strange tingling sensation over his whole body, and the hair on his skin seemed to rise. Father Jay was silent as he blessed the space, and Jose knew that the priest could sense the same eerie feeling he was experiencing. After thoroughly dousing the shed with holy water, Father Jay guided Jose out to the welcoming freshness of the outside air while remaining uncharacteristically quiet.

The two men reconnected with the other team members who were gathered near the pool, along with the rest of Jose's family. The team was confident that they had found the lair of the primary malevolent entity—the one that roamed the house at night, harassing and frightening the occupants. It was hidden in a very old and gnarled mango tree on the neighboring property. The branches of this rough and lumpy blackened tree stretched beyond the wall separating the two homes and hung menacingly over Jose's lot. Likewise, its roots had snaked under the wall, upending the earth and creating treacherous obstacles for Jose's family for as long as he could remember. But the real menace was the tree's inhabitant.

"It's a huge, hideous demon," Sister Rose told them in a somber voice. "It is covered in dark, hairy fur."

Once again, unaware as he was of the spirit realm and its workings, Jose found himself at a loss for words. He found it curious that the other team members seemed to accept the nun's statement as nothing too surprising. *Oh, a huge hairy demon is living in this tree. And how is the weather today?* It did bring to mind, though, rumors from his childhood about his long-deceased neighbors putting out bowls of food, alcohol, and cigarettes as offerings to the *engkanto*. But such superstitious practices were so common among his people that he never thought much of them.

Soon after the team's surprising discovery, Martin arrived with a large olive wood cross that Sister Rose had asked him to retrieve so it could be used as a weapon against the *kapre*, the tree demon. Almost half the size of an average person, the cross had been purchased in Jerusalem and blessed by Pope John Paul II. Additionally, it had touched numerous sacred sites during a pilgrimage Martin had once embarked on. It was Martin's prized possession, and as he handed it over to the nun, Jose knew his brother was probably a little nervous about what might happen to it. Then the group watched anxiously as the sister clutched the large crucifix tightly in front of her and walked toward the dark tree.

Jose will never forget what happened next.

The stout sister spun rapidly around like a whirling dervish! She struggled frantically to maintain her balance, teetering on the brink of falling into the pool just a step away. At the final moment, she found her footing and quickly moved back. Clearly shaken, she collapsed into a poolside chair.

Jose was still trying to comprehend what he had just witnessed. Did that really just happen? Did an invisible entity just pick up this large woman and twirl her around like a child's top? Jose looked at the others gathered around and saw the same shocked expression on their faces. Then he turned to Sister Rose and saw that she appeared to be regaining her composure and strength. She offered him a faint smile and asked him to carry the crucifix now that she was ready to continue her confrontation with the *kapre*. She reassured him that he had nothing to fear since he was a seminarian. Jose agreed to help, but in his heart, he was terrified. He recognized his status as a seminarian, but he felt the nun was overestimating the grace in his soul.

Then, in a resolute manner, Sister Rose stood up and handed Jose the large crucifix. He took it and held it firmly in front of his chest like a shield poised to deflect incoming spiritual arrows. And then he silently prayed that he would not become the target of any demonic retaliation. As he followed the sister to the mango tree, Jose suddenly noticed a surprising tranquility within himself. *This is what it feels like knowing God is on your side,* he thought. He could also tell that Sister Rose was better prepared this time, her stance and demeanor exuding confidence and determination. She promptly resumed her assault with swift and precise commands against the devilish fiend, her voice ringing out with authority. The demon was given no opportunity to strike back, though it weakly tried to manifest by rippling the pool water and shaking the branches of its poached tree. As inexperienced as he was, Jose could nonetheless feel that victory was close.

"In the name of Christ, begone!" Sister Rose commanded, her voice rising above the bluster of the shaking leaves. Over and over, she ordered the entity to leave until, finally, the tree seemed to shudder in place. Jose wasn't sure if it was his imagination, but he thought he saw *something*—a vague, blackish shape—materialize and then, just as quickly, dissipate into the wind. Sister Rose had no doubts. She told him that she saw a shadowy, dark beast flee from the tree. It was the demon, she said. Then, turning to the concerned group behind her, she announced joyfully and triumphantly that it was over.

Jose knew it was over because all the physical maladies that the sister had been afflicted with upon arrival were gone, including the mysterious rash on her arms. Her very appearance had transformed as well, and she now radiated youthful vitality and exuberance. In fact, the entire team's demeanor had changed, their formerly anxious and somber dispositions replaced by an air of peace and lively camaraderie.

As far as Jose could recall, there were no more reports of paranormal activity from the residents or staff of his childhood home. Interestingly, several months later a storm rolled in, and a powerful gust of wind ripped the ancient, twisted mango tree from the ground.

"One of the realities of being an exorcist is the retaliation of evil spirits. One morning, I woke up with a painful back. Since I had a full day ahead, I did not give it much thought. Later that same day, a lady walked into the parish requesting a 'pray-over' because of a bad back. This woman had an open third eye and had accidentally backed up her car to a bush, hurting the back of what she knew was a dwarf. Not only was the retaliation done on the lady but on me as well. The spirit knew who would be doing the 'pray-over.'"

– Fr. Ramon Merino, exorcist, Archdiocese of Manila

CHAPTER 13

The Foul Fiend

As the world emerged from the harrowing aftermath of World War II, the Berry family found themselves confronting a different kind of battle—one that challenged their understanding of reality and tested the limits of their faith. This conflict was not waged along geopolitical borders, nor against a visible foe, but rather against an insidious darkness lurking in a shadowy realm of existence where the boundaries between the ordinary and the extraordinary can become indistinguishable from one another.

* * *

In the summer of 1945, as Europe emerged from the scourge of World War II, British army physician Dr. Ian Berry looked to put the horrors of battle behind him by taking an extended retreat to his Belgian vacation home. Accompanied by his wife, Eleanor, and two young children, Matilda and James, Dr. Berry anticipated a season of respite and rejuvenation in the stately three-story dwelling. Tucked away in an idyllic country setting and attended to by two young Romanian maids, the grand estate seemed the perfect solution for the family to regain their bearings in a world recently turned upside down. They were soon to discover, however, that their private world was not yet ready to be righted, and that their long-anticipated peaceful getaway would be anything but.

Within weeks of their arrival, strange occurrences began to disrupt the household's peace. It started with banging in the walls, which at first Dr. Berry attributed to the "hammering" of plumbing lines when the taps were turned on and off. But this theory was quickly discarded when the noise continued in the middle of the night when no one was using any water. Other oddities included the rattling of dishes in kitchen cupboards and the opening and closing of doors by themselves. Trying again to be logical, Dr. Berry blamed the age of the house and its faulty airflow and drafts for causing such problems. To put his family at ease, the doctor called in plumbers and other tradesmen, but despite their best efforts, they could never find any obvious causes of these mysterious occurrences.

As the weeks passed, the disturbances intensified in both frequency and intensity. Objects, both small and large, seemed to move of their own accord. Chairs and lamps were found in different positions, and the household was gripped by a growing sense of unease. One evening, a porcelain vase flew across the room, narrowly missing Eleanor and shattering against the mantelpiece. Another night soon after, Matilda awoke screaming. Dr. Berry and Eleanor raced to her bedroom, where they found the terrified child huddled under her blankets, her entire collection of dolls and stuffed animals intricately piled up on her bed like a troupe of acrobats.

As fears arose and tensions heightened in the Berry household, suspicion was naturally cast upon the "strangers" in the house, 18-year-old twin sisters Adriana and Camelia, who had been hired as housekeepers a month before the Berrys arrived at the manor. Dr. Berry and Eleanor discussed privately the possibility of the sisters playing pranks on the family, but in many instances the maids themselves were either present for the strange phenomena or victims of it themselves. However, as time went on, one thing became increasingly clear: Adriana had an uncanny knack for always being present when the strange occurrences began, as well as being incredibly unflustered by any of it.

Dr. Berry, as much as he prided himself on his scientific knowledge and pragmatism, was not entirely closed to belief in the supernatural. Not only did he have some semblance of religious faith from his childhood upbringing in the Anglican church, but he also had witnessed many things during the war that he couldn't explain. With an open and curious mind, he began giving serious consideration to the idea that Adriana was somehow causing the disturbances, if not because of a pathological issue, then perhaps through some sort of extra-sensory ability. Determined to test his theory, Dr. Berry convinced Eleanor to go back to England with the children, arguing that it was already too dangerous to stay and that his further plans might make it more so. Then he called up two colleagues to help him.

With Adriana's consent, the doctors conducted an extensive series of tests, evaluations, and interviews with the young girl in the hopes of discovering something—anything—that could help explain the strange events of the past several weeks. But after exhausting all avenues of scientific inquiry, the doctors could only conclude that Adriana exhibited no physical or psychological abnormalities or abilities. Dr. Berry was left with one other explanation, one he left unsaid in the presence of his colleagues for fear of appearing insane, but now was quite certain of: Adriana was possessed. Not only did the thought plague him from the start, but it seemed to prove itself at one point during the testing procedures when he was alone with Adriana for just a few minutes. He had been jotting notes down in a journal when he looked back up and saw that the girl's pupils had become slitted like a snake's and were staring at him with such malevolence that he found it hard to breathe.

Through his contacts back in London, Dr. Berry was given the name of a Catholic exorcist, Father Vincent Davies, who immediately agreed to come out and assess the situation. Upon arrival, Father Davies listened to Dr. Berry's account of all that had happened thus far and then interviewed the sisters individually. He started with Camelia, who, either out of fear or guilt, opened up to the priest about her and her sister's upbringing, something she had never discussed with the Berrys.

She told him that she and Adriana had grown up in abject poverty in Romania. Their father was abusive to them, and their mother took her own life when the twins were fourteen. Desperate for a better life, Adriana began visiting an old woman who was reputed to be the village witch. The woman took Adriana under her wing and taught her the ways of black magic. Adriana practiced her craft day and night and soon became proficient in spell casting and fortune telling. Before long, their financial woes began to ease and their future looked a bit brighter. When their father died suddenly of an unknown ailment, no one shed a tear. Adriana told Camelia that it was his fate and that theirs lay beyond the border. That's when they secured their jobs at the Berry estate.

After hearing Camelia's story, Father Davies feared the worst. He had seen enough cases to know that involvement in the occult never ended well. He had to know one more thing, and so he gently asked, "Camelia, does your sister still practice witchcraft?"

As she wrung her hands in her lap, the girl looked up at him with tears in her eyes. "Oh, Father, whenever she tries now, something terrible happens to her. Her face changes, her voice changes. And she looks at me like she wants to kill me." She began sobbing inconsolably. "She's not my sister anymore!"

Father Davies comforted Camelia as best as he could and then went into another room where Adriana was waiting for her interview.

"Thank you for waiting," said Father Davies. "I'm a bit parched after talking to your sister. Let me get us some water before we begin."

He went behind Adriana to where a pitcher of water sat on a credenza and proceeded to pour two glasses. From his pocket he drew a small bottle of holy water and, hiding his actions with his body, poured a tiny amount into one of the glasses. He pocketed the vial and came around to sit with Adriana.

"Here we are," he said, handing her the glass with the holy water in it. "Now, then, shall we—"

Suddenly, the glass Adriana was holding went flying of its own accord across the room and shattered against the wall.

"Stupid priest," sneered Adriana in a voice that sounded a thousand years old. "Did you think you could fool us?"

Father Davies drew a crucifix out of his vest pocket and, holding it aloft, began reciting a prayer in Latin. Then, still in Latin, he commanded the spirit in Adriana to answer him, to which the voice replied:

"Mea est. Ego sum legionis."

She is mine. I am Legion.

Then the voice repeated the answer in Greek. Then in Hebrew.

Father Davies had all the proof he needed that Adriana was demonically possessed. He contacted his bishop back in London, as well as the bishop of Ghent, and after obtaining their permission to conduct a formal exorcism, he went forth with his preparations.

Camelia, for her part, had been working tirelessly to persuade her sister to renounce her occult practices in the days leading up to the event, taking advantage of their close sibling relationship during those times when Adriana was free of the demon's control. Without Adriana's consent, the exorcism could not be performed, and so it was with much relief and joy that she finally agreed to break her ties with witchcraft and avail herself of the ministry.

The ritual was a brutal marathon, with daily sessions lasting for hours over the course of two weeks. Adriana was restrained on her bed during each bout so as to not harm herself or others. Dr. Berry and his colleagues kept a careful watch over the proceedings and did their best to remain nonplussed as Adriana spewed foul language, spoke in tongues, thrashed about, and chillingly revealed intimate and embarrassing details of those present, things she could not possibly have known on her own.

Undeterred by the demon's antics, Father Davies, along with an assisting priest from the local parish, remained steadfast in their mission. Though verbally assaulted with curses, insults, and innuendos, they recited the words of deliverance in strong and steady voices. Their nimbleness in avoiding flying objects and wads of spit became a point of envy among the others present in the room, although not always did they escape being hit. When in need of spiritual fortification and added armaments, they would periodically retreat to the first-floor dining room to say Mass using a large wooden sideboard as an altar. Father Davies later recalled that saying Mass during the exorcism was like "walking through a brick wall," given the oppressive demonic presence and the constant barrage of verbal and psychological attacks.

On the day the demon finally revealed its name, a series of extraordinary events unfolded. The air grew cold and heavy, as if charged with an otherworldly energy. Adriana writhed and convulsed against her restraints as the room filled with the stench of decay. And then, in a moment that would forever be seared into the memories of those present, Adriana's body released a torrent of bodily fluids. The room became a cesspool of filth—the demon's final act of defiance. And then, just as suddenly as it had begun, the deluge ceased and a heavy silence descended upon the room. Adriana slumped against the pillows behind her and uttered weakly, "It's gone."

"Thanks be to God," Dr. Berry exclaimed. He moved toward Adriana to examine her and then stopped suddenly. "What was that?" he asked, a puzzled expression appearing on his face.

The others in the room heard it as well—the sound of spitting coming from the hallway. Dr. Berry and Father Davies walked out to the hall to investigate, and what they perceived astounded them. Despite nothing being visible to the eye, there was the unmistakable sound of someone, or something, spitting in a path down the staircase toward the front door. At the entryway of the door, the sound abruptly stopped.

Gingerly, the men descended the steps and discovered a substance resembling human saliva on every second or third step of the staircase, as well as one last little puddle in front of the door.

"It appears our foul little fiend has a flair for the dramatic," Father Davies said with a chuckle.

The spittle, when cleaned up, left behind dark scorch marks. Dr. Berry later sent samples of the substance out to a lab for analysis, and the results confirmed that the substance was indeed human saliva.

Remaining true to her word to steer clear of witchcraft and the occult, Adriana remained free of demonic influences, at least while in the employ of Dr. Berry. The twin sisters moved to West Germany a few years later.

Father Davies returned to London and continued there as an exorcist before his death in the mid-1960s. Dr. Berry and his family eventually sold their Belgian vacation home, as they could never completely put from their minds the events that took place in the summer of 1945. They chose instead a bucolic horse farm on the outskirts of Leeds to spend their holidays and eventual retirement.

Where no demons, spitting or otherwise, were known to reside.

"Where devils are concerned, materializations of disgusting objects, such as bile-like fluids and other ghastly and nauseating substances, are always a possibility. Their powers transcend the demons, and you have a real problem if a devil or devils have stepped in."

– John Zaffis, paranormal researcher/demonologist

Final Thoughts

Throughout human history, there have always been those who seek power, knowledge, and control through arcane and esoteric means. From ancient Greek oracles to modern-day Ouija boards, the methods may vary, but the intention remains the same: to become like a god by discovering and harnessing secret powers. It is the desire to conform the world to one's own will—or as the infamous 20th-century occultist Aleister Crowley put it, to "do what thou wilt."

But if the stories in this book have taught us anything, it's that the occult does not bring enlightenment and empowerment. It brings deceit, despair, and danger. The promise that you can impose your will on the world and others through mind power, cosmic energy, laws of nature, spells, and rituals is a con. What the occult invokes are evil spirits, and evil spirits—demons—do not and will never serve humans. Seeking power from them only grants them a license to subjugate and tyrannize the seeker.

It was a lie from the very beginning, when the serpent in the Garden of Eden promised, "You will be like God," and it is a lie now, whispered by the same voice as then.

Selected Bibliography

Amorth, Gabriele. *An Exorcist Explains the Demonic: The Antics of Satan and His Army of Fallen Angels*. Sophia Institute Press, 2016.

"Armor of God: Spiritual Warfare." *YouTube*, youtube.com/-@spiritualwarfareseries.

Bethea, Ryan, and Carlos Martins. *The Exorcist Files*. www.exorcistfiles.tv.

Blai, Adam. *Hauntings, Possessions, and Exorcism*. Emmaus Road Publishing, 2017.

Blai, Adam. *The Exorcism Files: True Stories of Demonic Possession*. Sophia Institute Press, 2022.

Chestnut, Debi. *Something Wicked: A Ghost Hunter Explores Negative Spirits*. Llewellyn Publications, 2016.

Cuadrante, Joy L. *The Exorcist Files*. Society of St. Paul, 2020.

"Exorcism and Dangers of the Occult." *Paranormal Podcast with Jim Harold*. https://jimharold.com/exorcism-and-dangers-of-the-occult-paranormal-podcast-727/

Fortea, Jose Antonio. *Interview With an Exorcist: An Insider's Look at the Devil, Demonic Possession, and the Path to Deliverance*. Ascension Press, 2006.

Gallagher, Richard. *Demonic Foes: My Twenty-Five Years as a Psychiatrist Investigating Possessions, Diabolic Attacks, and the Paranormal.* HarperOne, 2020.

Harris, Samantha E. *Fighting Malevolent Spirits.* Llewellyn Publications, 2014.

Holmes, Ellie Gardey. "Witchcraft, a Multi-Billion-Dollar Industry, Is Rapidly Evangelizing." *The American Spectator,* March 25, 2024.

Koch, Kurt E. *Between Christ and Satan.* Evangelization Publishers, 1961.

Lampert, Vincent. *Exorcism: The Battle against Satan and His Demons.* Emmaus Road Publishing, 2020.

Rossetti, Stephen. *Diary of an American Exorcist: Demons, Possession, and the Modern-Day Battle against Ancient Evil.* Sophia Institute Press, 2021.

Sarchie, Ralph, and Lisa Collier Cool. *Deliver Us from Evil: A New York City Cop Investigates the Supernatural.* St. Martin's Griffin, 2014.

Sawyer, J.W. *Deliver Us From Evil.* OmniMedia Publishing, 2009.

Syquia, Jose Francisco. *Exorcism: Encounters With the Paranormal and the Occult.* Society of St. Paul, 2006.

Zaffis, John. *Shadows of the Dark.* iUniverse, 2004.

About the Author

John Harker is a freelance journalist and ghostwriter who's been writing and publishing since the 1990s. His personal encounters with unexplainable phenomena have inspired him to explore strange, dark, and disturbing topics in both non-fiction and fiction. He lives with his family in eastern Washington, where the ghosts are dry and dusty.

Visit John's website at johnharkerbooks.com for updates on book releases, paranormal news, and other information.

Also by John Harker

Hell Unleashed: True Tales of Possession, Oppression and Other Satanic Havoc

Monsters and Maniacs: True Tales of Mystery and Horror

When Demons Attack: True Tales of Diabolic Encounters

Evil Unleashed: True Tales of Spells Gone to Hell and Other Occult Disasters

Demonic Dolls: True Tales of Terrible Toys

Ouija Board Nightmares: Terrifying True Tales

Ouija Board Nightmares 2: More True Tales of Terror

www.ingramcontent.com/pod-product-compliance
Lightning Source LLC
Chambersburg PA
CBHW071321130726
47996CB00002B/570